To Charlie and Nat

Many Blessings

Walt Walker

EXTRAORDINARY ENCOUNTERS
WITH *God*

EXTRAORDINARY ENCOUNTERS
WITH *God*

*How Famous People in History
Experienced God
in Unexpected Ways*

Walter L. Walker

VINE
BOOKS

SERVANT PUBLICATIONS
ANN ARBOR, MICHIGAN

Vine Books is an imprint of Servant Publications especially designed to serve evangelical
Christians.

Unless otherwise noted, Scripture references are from the New American Standard Bible, © The
Lockman Foundation 1960, 1962, 1968, 1971, 1973, 1975, 1977. Scripture references marked
KJV are from the Authorized King James Version of the Bible.

Published by Servant Publications
P.O. Box 8617
Ann Arbor, Michigan 48107

Cover design: PAZ Design Group, Salem, Oregon

97 98 99 00   10 9 8 7 6 5 4 3 2 1

Printed in the United States of America
ISBN 1-56955-001-8

Library of Congress Cataloging-in-Publication Data

Walker, Walter
Extraordinary encounters with God : how famous people in history experienced God in unex-
pected ways / Walter L. Walker.
    p.   cm.
Includes bibliographical references.
ISBN 1-56955-001-8
1. Christian biography.   2. Spiritual biography.   I. Title.
BR1702.W27   1997
270'.092'2—dc21
[B]   97-6218
                                                                   CIP

Contents

10. Jeanne la Pucelle, Joan of Arc
    1425–1431

11. Christopher Columbus, Mapmaker and Explorer
    1491, 1502

12. Blaise Pascal, Scientist and Mathematician
    November 23, 1654

13. John Wesley, Founder of the Methodist Church
    May 24, 1738

14. George Frideric Handel, Composer of *Messiah*
    September 15, 1741

15. George Washington, Captain, Virginia Militia
    July 7, 1755

16. George Washington, Commander of the Continental Army
    Winter 1777

17. Charles Grandison Finney, America's Greatest Evangelist
    October 10, 1821

18. Harriet Tubman, Engineer on the Underground Railroad
    1849–1864

19. Harriet Beecher Stowe, Author of *Uncle Tom's Cabin*
    February 2, 1851

20. Abraham Lincoln, Sixteenth President of the United States
    April 1865

21. George Washington Carver, Professor of the Peanut
    1915

Notes

Introduction

HISTORY IS LIKE A GREAT THEATRICAL PRODUCTION, the plot twisting and turning as different individuals come onstage to play out their respective parts. In so many instances throughout the drama a turning point in the story line has been caused by a dream, a vision, or some kind of supernatural experience. Extraordinary encounters with God have either brought certain people to center stage or greatly influenced the impact of those already in that position.

We'll never know, this side of eternity, how often or how thoroughly the Great Director has orchestrated each scene of the play. Personally, I suspect it is more than we have ever imagined and that the most extraordinary stories of divine encounters have never been written down or even told.

This is a collection of thirty-one short stories about famous people who were greatly influenced by a divine encounter, many of them at a critical point in history. It is hard, if not impossible, to actually verify such reports; nor have I tried to do so. For the most part, I've simply let people tell in their own words what they experienced, and, in my own words the effect the experience had on their lives and, in many cases, on the world in which we live today.

I greatly appreciate all the suggestions and contributions from good friends. Special thanks to Linda, my wife, for her constant encouragement, as well as to Bert Ghezzi, Vice President and Editorial Director of Servant Publications.

There is already a growing file of story ideas about other famous people who have had some kind of a divine encounter. If you have heard such a story and would like to tell me about it, I would love to hear from you. My address is:

Walter L. Walker
c/o Servant Publications, Inc.
P.O. Box 8617
Ann Arbor, MI 48107

Epimenides of Crete

*A*ncient Athens was a city of gods, full of hundreds of temples and shrines erected in their honor. The Athenians were prolific collectors of gods, gathering every deity they came across to ship or cart to Athens. Petronius, a first-century writer startled by the number of gods in the city, wrote, "It was easier to find a god in Athens than it was to find a man."

The following story of a divine encounter is taken primarily from the writing of a third-century Greek historian, Diogenes Laertius.[1]

At the beginning of the sixth century before Christ, only a few years before the Jews would be conquered by the Assyrians and taken into Babylonian captivity, Athens was stricken with a terrible plague that killed many of its citizens. Despite the lavish sacrifices made to the various gods, the plague continued to spread. One of the religious leaders declared that the city was under a curse for the crimes of King Megacles. He had granted amnesty to the followers of one of his enemies, then broke his promise and proceeded to execute them all. Since, however, the people of Athens had sacrificed to every god they knew, the religious leader concluded that there must be an unknown god who was still offended by Megacles' atrocities. The ruling council decided to follow this leader's advice. Diogenes Laertius wrote that it was "in the 46th Olympiad [595–592 B.C.]" when the council sent a ship commanded by Nicias to Cnossus on the island of Crete to summon the great and wise philosopher Epimenides.

Arriving in Athens, Epimenides was astounded by the number of gods and idols throughout the city. Yet it was his task to identify the one god who had not yet been reconciled to the Athenians. Brought to Mars Hill to stand before the assembled elders of Athens, who thanked him for coming, Epimenides replied:

> Learned elders of Athens, there is no need to thank me. Tomorrow at sunrise bring a flock of sheep, a band of stone masons, and a large supply of stones and mortar to the grassy slope at the foot of this sacred rock. The sheep must all be healthy, and of different colors—some white, some black. And you must prevent them from grazing after their night's rest. They must be hungry sheep! I will now rest from my journey. Call me at dawn.[2]

Very early the next morning the hungry sheep, the stone masons, and hundreds of onlookers gathered on the slopes at the base of Mars Hill. The learned Epimenides stated that he was going to offer sacrifices based on three assumptions: 1) that there is still another god whose name is unknown to us, who is not represented by any of the idols in your city; 2) that this god is great enough and good enough to do something about the plague; and 3) that any god great enough and good enough to stop the plague is also great enough and good enough to smile upon people in their ignorance—if they acknowledge their ignorance and call upon him.

Epimenides ordered that the sheep, both the black and the white sheep, be released and allowed to graze and that each sheep was to be followed and watched. He then prayed aloud to the unknown god, acknowledging the people's ignorance and asking the god to reveal his willingness to help them by causing either the black or the white sheep to lie down. Those sheep he chose, Epimenides said, would be sacrificed.

It must have seemed a foolhardy prayer to the bystanders. The sheep seemed eager to graze, and everyone knew that no sheep would lie down to rest until its belly was full. To everyone's amazement, however, one by one the white sheep buckled their knees and lay down. On the spot where each one had rested, the stone masons built an altar. Epimenides ordered that no name be assigned to this god, but that there should be only an admission of ignorance. And so, the masons engraved on each altar *agnosto theo*—"to an unknown god."

The Athenians sacrificed the sheep on the altars as the Cretan philosopher had prescribed. By dawn the next day the plague had ceased to spread. By the end of one week no new cases were reported, and those already sick had recovered.

Athens was filled with praise for Epimenides and the "unknown god." They even built a statue of Epimenides and placed it in front of one of their temples.[3]

Over the centuries the altars deteriorated, but were not totally forgotten. Pausanias, a writer in the second century A.D., mentioned the "altars to an unknown god" (*Description of Greece*, I, 1:4), as did Philostratus in the early third century A.D. in his *Apollonius of Tyana*. At least one of the altars was surviving in approximately A.D. 45 when the Apostle Paul made his first visit to idol-infested Athens. The New Testament Book of Acts says that Paul's spirit "was being provoked within him as he was beholding the city full of idols" (Acts 17:16). The Acts account goes on to say that Paul, who was surely trained in classical history and literature, "reasoned in the synagogue" with the Athenian Jews…and "in the marketplace" with the Athenian Gentiles, concerning the gospel of Jesus Christ. Some of the Epicurean and Stoic philosophers heard Paul and decided to bring him to the Areopagus on Mars Hill to be heard by the council. Standing before them, Paul said,

> Men of Athens, I observe that you are very religious in all respects. For while I was passing through and examining the objects of your worship, I also found an altar with this inscription, "TO AN UNKNOWN GOD." What therefore you worship in ignorance, this I proclaim to you. The God who made the world and all things in it, since He is Lord of heaven and earth, does not dwell in temples made with hands; neither is He served by human hands, as though He needed anything, since He Himself gives to all life and breath and all things. ACTS 17:22–25

Did the surviving altar with the inscription "To an Unknown God" merely serve as a convenient illustration for the Apostle Paul? Or did Paul intend to make reference to the history of Athens and, particularly, to Epimenides? Apparently, Paul was indeed intending to remind the Athenians of this divine encounter in their past. Continuing his address, Paul said:

[God] hath made of one blood all nations of men for to dwell on all the face of the earth, and hath determined the times before appointed, and the bounds of their habitation; that they should seek the Lord, if haply they might feel after him, and find him, though he be not far from every one of us: for in him we live, and move, and have our being; as certain also of your own poets have said. ACTS 17:26–28, KJV

Paul quoted from one of their own poets—the poet named Epimenides! A quatrain from one of Epimenides' poems reads:

They fashioned a tomb for thee, O holy and high one—
The Cretans, always liars, evil beasts, idle bellies!
But thou art not dead; thou livest and abidest for ever;
For in thee we live and move and have our being.[4]

The second line of the same quatrain is found in Paul's Letter to Titus: "One of themselves, even a prophet of their own, said, 'The Cretans are always liars, evil beasts, slow bellies'" (Titus 1:12, KJV). Paul was obviously familiar with the writing of Epimenides, and he used the story of his divine encounter as the starting point of his message to the Athenians.

Alexander the Great

KING OF MACEDONIA
SPRING 334 B.C.

*A*lexander was born in 356 B.C., the son of Philip, King of Macedonia. Philip had in only twenty years transformed a nation of peasants and shepherds into a unified military state. He had succeeded in subjugating the Greek city-states and from this base of power hoped to undertake the conquest of Asia.[1]

Alexander inherited the ambition of his father. On one occasion he wept bitterly upon hearing of his father's conquests and said, "My father will get ahead of me in everything and will leave nothing great for me to do."[2]

Alexander's mother, Olympias, was brilliant as well as hot-tempered. She was determined that her son would have the best education. When he was fourteen, Alexander became the pupil of Aristotle, who impressed upon his young student that he could rule the world if he could make people adopt the Greek language and culture.[3] Olympias had taught her son that Achilles was his ancestor, and that his father was descended from Hercules. Alexander learned the stories of Achilles from Homer's *Iliad*, a copy of which he always carried with him. He knew the story by heart, and Achilles became his model in all things.[4]

When he was only eighteen years old, Alexander commanded part of his father's cavalry at the battle of Chaeronea. In 337, King Philip died, leaving the Macedonian kingdom to the twenty-year-old Alexander. Philip had once said to Alexander, "O my son, seek out a kingdom worthy of thyself, for Macedonia is too little for thee."[5]

Alexander, now in full control of the military power his father had created, sat in Macedonia pondering how he could conquer the nations and rule the world. According to Josephus, the first-century Jewish historian, Alexander was told in a dream to boldly cross the Aegean Sea without delay, and that he would be given victory over the Persians.[6] The dream was significant in a military sense because it was what started Alexander on his world conquest. Later on the dream was also to have a great religious significance because of the appearance of the man in his dream, and particularly because of how he was dressed.

In those days the Persian Empire under King Darius III dominated Palestine and extended to the eastern edge of Asia Minor. Alexander crossed the Hellespont (modern-day Dardanelles), the strait separating Macedonia from Asia Minor (modern-day Turkey), and defeated the Persian forces. He continued thereafter along the Mediterranean coast all the way to Syria. Hearing of the Persian defeat in Asia Minor and of Alexander's march into Syria, Darius III raised a huge army to stop him before he conquered all of southern Asia. It was generally assumed that the Macedonians would not even engage the battle, because of the great multitude of the Persian army. But Alexander marched north and routed the Persians, even overrunning Darius' camp. The Persian king's wife and mother were captured, while Darius barely escaped.[7]

Alexander returned south to Syria and besieged the city of Tyre for seven months. Part of the city of Tyre was located on the coastal plain and the other part on an offshore island, and it was to this island that the population fled. Not to be thwarted, Alexander constructed a causeway so that the island became a peninsula and remains so to this day.

While at Tyre, Alexander sent a message to the Jewish high priest in Jerusalem, one hundred miles to the south. The priest was to send supplies for the Macedonian army. In addition, whatever tribute had formerly been paid to Darius III should now be sent to Alexander. He added that choosing to support the Macedonian cause would be a decision the high priest would not regret.[8] But Jaddua, the high priest, answered that he had given an oath to Darius not to bear arms against him and that he would not violate that oath while Darius was still alive. Alexander, not accustomed to such refusals, determined that when the siege of Tyre was completed, he would make an expedition against Jerusalem. He warned that "through him [Jaddua]" he would "teach all men to whom they must keep their oaths!"

Having defeated Gaza as well as Tyre, Alexander hurriedly marched toward Jerusalem to make an example of that city and its rebellious high priest. What happened when he arrived was both astonishing and completely unexpected. The following is a paraphrase of an account by Josephus of Alexander's arrival at Jerusalem:

Jaddua the high priest, when he heard that Alexander was approaching Jerusalem, was terrified and in great agony, not knowing how he should meet the Macedonians since Alexander was so enraged at his disobedience. Therefore, he ordered that the people join him in offering sacrifices to God, hoping that God would protect the nation. After having offered the sacrifices, God instructed Jaddua in a dream that he should take courage, adorn the city, and open the gates to the Macedonians. He and the priests, according to the dream, were to appear in white garments, and neither he nor the priests should meet Alexander with the dread of any ill consequences, for the providence of God would prevent it.

Jaddua arose from his sleep, greatly rejoiced, and declared to all the dream he had received from God. He did everything exactly as he was instructed by God in the dream, and waited for the coming of Alexander. When Jaddua understood that Alexander was not far away, he went out from the city leading a procession of priests and a multitude of citizens.

Because of Alexander's anger against Jaddua and the Jews, the Phoenicians and Chaldeans who followed Alexander thought surely they would be allowed to plunder the city and torment the high priest to death. The reverse happened.

The multitude of Jews approached the Macedonian army in white garments, with the priests clothed in fine linen. The high priest wore a purple and scarlet garment with the mitre on his head, having the golden plate on which the name of God was engraved. When Alexander saw this, he approached by himself, bowed, and saluted the high priest. The Jews all together with one voice then saluted Alexander and surrounded him.

The kings of Syria, the commanders, and all who followed Alexander were astounded at what he had done, supposing that he had become "disordered in his mind." However, Parmenio, who was Alexander's most favored general, went up to Alexander and asked how it had come to pass, since he was adored by all others, that he should bow down to the high priest of the Jews?

To Parmenio he replied, "I did not bow down to him but to the God who hath honored him with His high priesthood, for I saw this very person in a dream, in this very dress when I was at Dios in Macedonia considering with myself how I might obtain the dominion of Asia. In the dream he exhorted me to make no delay, but to boldly pass over the sea thither, for he would conduct my army and would give me the dominion over the Persians. Having seen no other such person in that dress and now seeing this person in it and remembering that vision and the exhortations which I had in my dream, I believe that I bring this army under divine conduct and shall therewith conquer Darius and destroy the power of the Persians."

Having said this to Parmenio, Alexander gave his right hand to the high priest. The priests ran along beside them until they came into the city and went up into the temple. Alexander offered sacrifices to God according to the high priest's directions, and treated both the high priest and the other priests magnificently.

Then the book of Daniel was shown to Alexander, in particular, the place where Daniel interpreted Nebuchadnezzar's dream of the great statue. Daniel interpreted the dream to mean that a Greek would destroy and replace the empire of the Persians. Alexander concluded that he was that person.[9]

From there Alexander proceeded into Egypt, and since the Egyptians hated the harsh rule of the Persians, he was welcomed as a deliverer. Alexander founded a city just west of the Nile Delta on the island of Pharos. This city, Alexandria, became the world's great center of learning and commerce. Afterwards, Alexander again turned against Persia and in 331 defeated Darius III at Arbela near the modern-day city of Irbil, Iraq. The Battle of Arbela is considered one of the fifteen most decisive battles in history.[10]

Alexander invited Jews to come live in the city of Alexandria. It was there that the Hebrew Scriptures were translated into Greek. This Greek translation, called the Septuagint, became "the Scriptures" of the early Christian church. Though his kingdom was divided among his generals soon after his death at the age of thirty-three, Alexander's legacy was that he hellenized the entire world. So thoroughly were the nations conquered culturally by the Greeks that Rome itself became a Greek-speaking city. Juvenal, one of the famous satirists of his day, complained, "I cannot, fellow Romans, bear a city wholly Greek."[11] It was in great measure due to the common language throughout the Roman Empire that Christianity was able to spread throughout the world so quickly.

THREE

Abgarus
KING OF EDESSA
CIRCA A.D. 40

*A*round the time of Christ, Abgar Ucomo (or Abgar the Black) reigned as king of Edessa. Edessa was a city of Northern Mesopotamia, near the River Euphrates. Abgarus was described as having reigned with "great glory." However, it was also said that he was wasting away from a dreadful and incurable disease. Having heard frequent rumors of the Jew named Jesus whose miracles were unanimously attested to by all, Abgarus sent a message by means of a letter carrier.

According to Eusebius, a third-century historian, a copy of the letter from Abgarus to Jesus was kept in the public records of the city of Edessa. The letter, which Eusebius "literally translated from the Syriac language, opportunely as we hope, and without profit," read:

Abgarus, prince of Edessa, sends greetings to Jesus the excellent Saviour, who has appeared in the borders of Jerusalem. I have heard the reports respecting thee and thy cures, as performed by thee with medicines and without the use of herbs. For as it is said, thou causest the blind to see again, the lame to walk, and thou cleanest the lepers…and thou raiseth the dead. And hearing all these things of thee, I conclude in my mind one of two things: either that thou art God, and having descended from heaven, doest these things, or else doing them, thou art the son of God. Therefore, now I have written and besought thee to visit me, and to heal the disease with which I am afflicted. I have, also, heard that the Jews murmur against thee, and are plotting to injure thee; I have, however, a very small but noble state, which is sufficient for us both.

Abgarus, Prince of Edessa[1]

Eusebius also chronicled the existence of the written response sent by Jesus to King Abgarus by the same letter carrier, which also was kept in the archives of the city:

Blessed art thou, O Abgarus, who, without seeing, hast believed in me. For it is written concerning me, that they who have seen me will not believe, that they who have not seen, may believe and live. But in regard to what thou hast written, that I should come to thee, it is necessary that I should fulfill all things here, for which I have been sent. And after this fulfillment, thus to be received again by Him that sent me. And after I have been received up, I will send to thee a certain one of my disciples, that he may heal thy afflictions, and give life to thee and to those who are with thee.

Jesus of Nazareth[2]

Eusebius stated that there was attached to these letters an account of what eventually happened:

After the ascension of Jesus, Judas, who is also called Thomas, sent him Thaddeus, the apostle, one of the seventy;…Thaddeus, therefore, began in the power of God to heal every kind of disease and infirmity; so that all were amazed. But when Abgarus heard the great deeds and miracles which he performed, and how he healed men in the name and power of Jesus Christ, he began to suspect that this was the very person concerning whom Jesus had written….

When he (Thaddeus) came, his nobles were present, and stood around. Immediately on his entrance, something extraordinary appeared to Abgarus, in the countenance of the apostle Thaddeus; which Abgarus observing, paid him reverence. But all around were amazed; for they did not perceive the vision which appeared to Abgarus alone….

Then said Thaddeus, "Therefore, I place my hand upon thee in the name of the same Lord Jesus." And this being done, he was immediately healed of the sickness and sufferings with which he was afflicted.[3]

Thaddeus refused to accept the silver and gold offered as compensation, but asked that the entire city be gathered to hear the gospel of Jesus.

There is naturally some dispute with regard to the authenticity of the correspondence, with experts supporting both sides. In 1846 an ancient Syriac manuscript was discovered documenting the earliest establishment of Christianity in Edessa from the first century to the fourth century. In the introduction Dr. William Cureton said, "I have found amongst the Syriac manuscripts in the British Museum a considerable portion of the original Aramaic document which Eusebius cites as preserved in the archives of Edessa." The document goes into great detail about Thaddeus' visit to Edessa and how the city turned to Christianity as the result of the great miracle.[4]

Saul of Tarsus

APOSTLE OF JESUS CHRIST TO THE GENTILES

CIRCA A.D. 35

Saul of Tarsus was one of those leaders who come along about once a century, destined to be great at something. What such a man eventually accepts as the challenge of his life depends largely on the times and circumstances into which he is born. But the natural course of a person's life sometimes takes a radical turn as the result of a divine encounter. An encounter with God so dramatic and so life-transforming is often referred to as a "Damascus Road experience." The term comes from an event in the life of Saul of Tarsus that not only altered his life but the course of history as well.

Saul was raised as a devout Jew in Tarsus, in what is today southern Turkey. He was raised in the Greek culture that had permeated the entire Roman Empire, and he was therefore a "Hellenistic" Jew—a Greek–speaking Jew living outside of Palestine. Saul received his formal education at the feet of Gamaliel, a renowned teacher of Old Testament Law and the traditions of the scribes. He became a member of the most conservative and zealous sect of Judaism, the Pharisees.

Pharisees were what you might call the "religious right" of their day. As members of the Sanhedrin, the ruling council of the Jews, they had a strong voice in politics. They were radical conservatives who resisted the corrupting influences of the Greek culture that was being force-fed to the people of Judea by Rome. The top-ranking Roman in Palestine was a career bureaucrat named Pontius Pilate.

Jesus of Nazareth never got along very well with the Pharisees. In their zeal to keep the Law of Moses, they had added to it thousands of regulations which, in their understanding, were applications of the Law to every aspect and activity of life. They were blind to the fact that they had made religion a heavy burden and that they had missed the main point altogether. Jesus' criticism of the Pharisees finally did Him in, and they arranged for Him to be crucified by Pilate.

Soon after His crucifixion Jesus' followers claimed that He had risen and presented Himself among them on numerous occasions. The tomb was indeed empty, even though it had been guarded by Roman soldiers around the clock. Those who believed that Jesus was risen from the dead and was indeed the promised Messiah (or the Christ) formed a sect within Judaism known as the Way.

There is no record of Saul of Tarsus ever coming in direct contact with Jesus before His crucifixion. Jesus was so immensely popular, at least among the common people, however, that Saul would certainly have kept informed of His message and His movements, as did the other Pharisees.

After Christ's crucifixion, Saul definitely came into great conflict with His followers. By A.D. 35 Saul was in Jerusalem and most probably a member of a Greek-speaking synagogue called "The Synagogue of the Freedmen." Many of the Hellenistic Jews in Jerusalem were becoming believers in Jesus as the Jewish Messiah.

The message of His resurrection had surely made deep inroads into Saul's Hellenistic synagogue. Saul reacted to this violently. This Jesus was a criminal, convicted and shamefully crucified. How dare anyone suggest that He was the Jewish Messiah!

Finally, the controversy came to a head. A member of the Hellenistic synagogue, a believer named Stephen, was falsely accused of blasphemy, dragged before the council, convicted, and stoned to death. Saul stood and watched, perhaps even supervising as the instigator. Stephen became the first martyr of the church.

Immediately after Stephen's death a great persecution of the church began, primarily under the direction of Saul. Having been commissioned with authority from the chief priest, he and the men under his authority would go from house to house looking for men and women who were believers. Once the believers were imprisoned, Saul tried to force them to blaspheme, and as Saul himself said, "When they were being put to death I cast my vote against them" (Acts 26:10).

Saul would pursue those who fled, to bring them back to prison. One of the most historic divine encounters took place as Saul was on his way to Damascus, commissioned by the chief priests to capture members of this sect called the Way. In Saul's own words:

And it came about that as I was on my way, approaching Damascus about noontime, a very bright light suddenly flashed from heaven all around me, and I fell to the ground and heard a voice saying to me, "Saul, Saul, why are you persecuting Me?" And I answered, "Who art Thou, Lord?" And He said to me, "I am Jesus the Nazarene, whom you are persecuting." And those who were with me beheld the light, to be sure, but did not understand the voice of the One who was speaking to me. And I said, "What shall I do, Lord?" And the Lord said to me, "Arise and go on into Damascus; and there you will be told of all that has been appointed for you to do." But since I could not see because of the brightness of the light, I was led by the hand by those who were with me, and came into Damascus. And a certain Ananias, a man who was devout by the standard of the Law, and well spoken of by all the Jews who lived there, came to me, and standing near said to me, "Brother Saul, receive your sight!" And at that very time I looked up at him. And he said, "The God of our fathers has appointed you to know His will, and to see the Righteous One, and to hear an utterance from His mouth. For you will be a witness for Him to all men of what you have seen and heard."   ACTS 22:6–15

Saul did indeed become a witness. He adopted a Greek name, Paul, and made Antioch his base of operations. It was in Antioch that the believers were first called "Christians." Through the Apostle Paul's missionary expeditions, the gospel of Jesus Christ spread throughout the Roman Empire and the entire world. The hinge-point in the history of Western civilization was Saul's divine encounter on the Damascus Road which transformed him from a persecutor of the church to the Apostle of Jesus Christ to the Gentiles.

FIVE

Flavius Valerius Constantinus
EMPEROR OF ROME
OCTOBER 27, A.D. 312

The Emperor Diocletian governed the Roman Empire with an iron fist for twenty-one years. He was a fanatic for efficiency, and in time he became increasingly irritable and suspicious of anything that kept the empire from running smoothly. There was no place in the Roman state for dissent or disagreement. This, of course, caused things to go poorly for Christians who refused to worship the ancient gods of the Empire. This refusal brought their loyalty to Rome into question.

Flavius Constantinus, or Constantine as he is more commonly known, was a member of the emperor's household. He was probably present at heated dinner-table debates about Christianity. Diocletian's wife and daughter had both become Christians. On the other hand, Caesar Galerius, the son of a barbarian priestess, angrily opposed Christianity.

In A.D. 303 Diocletian issued an order that all Christians were to sacrifice to the official pagan god. After a zealous young Christian ripped down the posted edict, all hell broke loose. Three of Diocletian's most senior staff who had become Christians were executed, as well as the local bishop. Many others fearlessly endured the most excruciating tortures. The religious crackdown came to be known as the Great Persecution.

Constantine witnessed many of these feats of Christian courage, which no doubt made a significant impression on him. But he made no outward show of sympathy for Christians or faith in Christ. He continued to offer the prescribed sacrifices and worship Mithras, the Sun-god of the Roman soldiers. Caesar Galerius was his political rival and would have jumped at any opportunity to indict Constantine of treason.

Under the persecution begun by Diocletian, Christians were hunted, burned, thrown to wild beasts, and put to death by every torture that cruelty could devise. Two years after the persecution began, Diocletian abdicated and pronounced Caesar Galerius emperor of the Eastern Empire, and Chlorus, Constantine's father, ruler in the West. As you would expect, Galerius continued the Great Persecution in the East. Caesar Chlorus, however, refused to carry out Diocletian's persecution against the Christians in the West.

It was becoming increasingly dangerous for Constantine. Galerius hated him and was very jealous of his popularity. Constantine made a clever and daring escape and joined his father, who was leading a campaign in Gaul.

After only about a year and a half, Chlorus died. As had happened on several occasions in the previous century, the Roman legions proclaimed their dead leader's son the new emperor. The news spread quickly, and soon the western provinces joined in proclaiming Constantine emperor.

Over the next six years there was a tremendous amount of political and military posturing. The Christians rejoiced when in 311 Galerius died, after which a political free-for-all ensued. At one point there were four emperors and several other claimants to the throne.

In the autumn of 312, Constantine, having declared himself emperor of the West, advanced with his legions on the city of Rome. The city was occupied by Galerius' successor, the Roman general Maxentius, whose troops had also proclaimed him emperor.

Constantine's scouts reported that the city seemed impregnable. Concealing his fears about what lay ahead of them, he ordered the legions to camp for the night eight miles from the city. On October 27, 312, the day before the Battle of Milvian Bridge, Constantine had a marvelous encounter. There is no written account by Constantine himself of what happened that night. Eusebius gives two accounts of the story, the first in his *Ecclesiastical History* and another in his *Life of Constantine*. Eusebius claims Constantine told him this story and swore to it by an oath.

He (Constantine) called on God with earnest prayer and supplications that he would reveal to him who he was, and stretch forth his right hand to help him in his present difficulties. And while he was thus praying with fervent entreaty, a most marvelous sign appeared to him from heaven, the account of which it might have been hard to believe had it been related by any other person. But since the victorious emperor himself long afterwards declared it to the writer of this history, when he was honored with his acquaintance and society, and confirmed his statement by an oath, who could hesitate to accredit the relation, especially since the testimony of after-time has established its truth? He said that about noon, when the day was already beginning to decline, he saw with his own eyes the trophy of a cross of light in the heavens, above the sun, and bearing the inscription, "Conquer by This Sign" [*In Hoc Signo Vinces*]. At this sight he himself was struck with amazement, and his whole army also, which followed him on this expedition, and witnessed the miracle.

He said, moreover, that he doubted within himself what the import of this apparition could be. And while he continued to ponder and reason on its meaning, night suddenly came on; then in his sleep the Christ of God appeared to him with the same sign which he had seen in the heavens, and commanded him to make a likeness of that sign which he had seen in the heavens, and to use it as a safeguard in all engagement with his enemies.[1]

Constantine ordered that the Greek letters Chi and Rho (the first two letters in the Greek word for Christ) be painted on the helmets and shields of his soldiers. These two Greek letters look like the English letters *X* and *P*, and appeared as in the following illustration:

Like that of the Apostle Paul, to whom Jesus appeared while he was traveling on the road to Damascus, the vision was so vivid to Constantine that he became a Christian.

Constantine's legions won a great victory on the following day, and he became the first Christian Roman emperor. October 28, A.D. 312 was the most significant turning point in European history.

Augustine of Hippo

PHILOSOPHER AND THEOLOGIAN

SUMMER A.D. 386

*A*urelius Augustine was born in A.D. 354 in the city of Thagaste in what is today Algeria. Over the centuries Augustine has emerged as the most formative theologian of the church after the Apostle Paul. He is revered by both Protestants and Catholics. Even though the North African world in which Augustine lived is now dominated by Islam, he is still recognized there as "Runi Kabar," "The Great Christian."

Augustine lived during a time when the glorious Roman Empire would quickly go into decline. At his birth most people could have easily imagined that the Empire would go on and prosper—if not for a thousand years, at least for all the foreseeable future. Sixty years after Augustine's death, however, the Empire had deteriorated beyond recognition.

Though Augustine's parents were not rich, they insisted that he have an education. His father, Patricius, was pagan, but his mother, Monica, was a woman of such piety that she is herself one of the most revered women in the history of the Christian church.

Augustine was educated in rhetoric (law) at the University of Carthage, where he was known for his wild lifestyle. While in Carthage Augustine joined a heretical sect called the Manichaeans whose beliefs were based on a dualistic philosophy. All sin was blamed on the evil nature within, which no one could help and for which no one was responsible. This "no-guilt religion" fit Augustine's lifestyle perfectly. He tells how he became so attached to Manichaeism:

> I always used to win more arguments than was good for me, debating with unskilled Christians who had tried to stand up for their faith in argument. With this quick succession of triumphs, the hot-headedness of a young man soon hardened into pig-headedness. As for this technique of argument, because I had set out on it after I had become a "Hearer" (among the Manichees), whatever I picked up by my own wits or by reading I willingly ascribed to the effects of their teaching. And so, from their preaching, I gained an enthusiasm for religious controversy, and for this I daily grew to love the Manichees more and more. So it came about that, to a surprising extent, I came to approve of whatever they wanted to be true.

In 373 Augustine, now in Milan, came upon some of the works of Cicero, which inflamed in him the love of philosophy that would burn throughout the rest of his life. He was particularly attracted to the writings of Plato. Gradually the professor of rhetoric began to have his doubts about the validity of Manichaeism. Also in Milan he came in contact with the great Ambrose, bishop of Milan, whose skills in rhetoric, philosophy, and Scripture were legendary. Thirdly, Augustine's mother joined him in Milan. Monica has been known throughout history as the mother who pleaded with, prayed for, and never gave up on her son. Ambrose's preaching, Monica's praying, the writings of St. Paul, and the Platonic ideal of personal integrity were beginning to get to Augustine.

As the years went by Augustine became more restless, more discontent, and filled with such inner turmoil that it overshadowed everything else in his life. At one point he was walking along one of the streets of Milan and noticed a beggar who had somehow gotten his fill of food and drink. The beggar was laughing and joking. He had found a happiness that Augustine felt was beyond his grasp. He later recalled:

> For by all my laborious contriving and intricate maneuvers I was hoping to win the joy of worldly happiness, the very thing which this man had already secured at the cost of a few pence which he had begged.[1]

Augustine devotes many chapters in his *Confessions* to the agony and crisis of his own soul. He also tells of an encounter in the summer of 386 that was, for him, his answer:

> There was a small garden attached to the house were we lodged.... I now found myself driven by the tumult in my breast to take refuge in this garden, where no one could interrupt that fierce struggle, in which I was my own contestant, until it came to its conclusion.... I tore my hair and hammered my forehead with my fists.... I locked my fingers and hugged my knees.[2]

I probed the hidden depths of my soul and wrung its pitiful secrets from it, and when I mustered them all before the eyes of my heart, a great storm broke within me, bringing with it a great deluge of tears. I stood up and left Alypius so that I might weep and cry to my heart's content, for it occurred to me that tears were best shed in solitude. So I stood up and left him where we had been sitting, utterly bewildered. Somehow I flung myself down beneath a fig tree and gave way to the tears. I had much to say to you, my God, not in these very words but in this strain: Lord, will you never be content? Must we always taste your vengeance? Forget the long record of our sins. For I felt that I was still the captive of my sins, and in my misery I kept crying "How long shall I go on saying 'Tomorrow, tomorrow'? Why not now? Why not make an end of my ugly sins at this moment?"

I was asking myself these questions, weeping all the while with the most bitter sorrow in my heart, when all at once I heard the sing-song voice of a child. Whether it was the voice of a boy or a girl I cannot say, but again and again it repeated the refrain, "Take it and read, take it and read." At this I looked up, thinking hard whether there was any kind of game in which children used to chant words like these, but I could not remember ever hearing them before. I stemmed my flood of tears and stood up, telling myself this could only be a divine command to open my book of Scripture and read the first passage on which my eyes should fall…. So I hurried back to the place were Alypius was sitting, for when I stood up to move away I had put down the book containing Paul's Epistles. I seized it and opened it, and in silence I read the first passage on which my eyes fell:

"Not in revelling and drunkenness, not in lust and wantonness, not in quarrels and rivalries. Rather, arm yourselves with the Lord Jesus Christ; spend no more thought on nature and nature's appetites." I had no wish to read more and no need to do so. For in an instant, as I came to the end of the sentence, it was as though the light of confidence flooded into my heart and all the darkness of doubt was dispelled.[3]

Augustine and his friend Alypius were baptized into the Christian faith by Ambrose himself. Augustine, Alypius, Monica, and a new Christian from Augustine's hometown of Thagaste decided to move back home to North Africa, where he would eventually serve more than thirty years as the bishop of Hippo. They were delayed in Italy, however, because of an impending civil war. During their stay in the town of Ostia at the mouth of the Tiber River, Monica and Augustine engaged in long conversations about experiencing the presence of God. Augustine describes one of those conversations:

As the flames of love burned stronger in us and raised us higher towards the eternal God, our thoughts ranged over the whole compass of material things in their various degrees, up to the heavens themselves, from which the sun and the moon and the stars shine down upon the earth…. Higher still we climbed, thinking and speaking all the while in wonder at all that you have made. At length we came to our own souls and passed beyond them to that place of everlasting plenty…. There life is that Wisdom by which all these things that we know are made, all things that ever have been and all that are yet to be.... And while we spoke of the eternal Wisdom, longing for it and straining for it with all the strength of our hearts, for one fleeting instant we reached out and touched it.[4]

At the end of their time together Monica said to Augustine:

My son, for my part I find no further pleasure in this life. What I am still to do or why I am here in the world, I do not know, for I have no more to hope for on this earth. There was one reason, and one alone, why I wished to remain a little longer in this life, and that was to see you a Christian before I died. God has granted my wish and more besides, for I now see you as his servant, spurning such happiness as the world can give. What is left for me to do in this world?[5]

Two weeks later Monica died. She had told her sons that she didn't care where she was buried. She was unconcerned about having an elaborate funeral or even a monument stone. Nevertheless, they did mark her grave. In 1945 two boys playing in a small courtyard beside the Church of St. Aurea in that city were digging a hole to plant a post for a game they were playing. They uncovered a fragment of marble that turned out to be Monica's tombstone, still bearing part of the original inscription.[6]

Patrick
PATRON SAINT OF IRELAND
A.D. 432

"*P*atrick" is the English form of the Latin name Patricius. The future patron saint of Ireland was born and raised in Roman Britain. At the age of sixteen, however, he was taken from his father's farm by raiders, carried to Ireland, and put to work tending sheep for the chieftain in Ulster. Six arduous years of slavery did not break the young man's spirit but turned Patrick into a devout Christian who prayed constantly. Later he wrote:

> After I had come to Ireland I daily used to feed cattle, and I prayed frequently during the day; the love of God and the fear of Him increased more and more…. I used even to remain in the woods and in the mountain; before daylight I used to rise to prayer, through snow, through frost, through rain, and felt no harm; nor was there any slothfulness in me, as I now perceive, because the spirit was then fervent within me.[1]

Patrick wrote of one particular night when, in his sleep, he heard a voice saying, "Thou fastest well, thou shalt soon go to thy country."

The promise was soon after repeated in another dream, but this time with more specific instructions: "Behold, thy ship is ready."

Patrick was told that the ship was more than two hundred miles away in a place he had never been, where there was no one he had ever known. He wrote in his autobiographical account:

> After this I took flight, and left the man with whom I had been six years; and I came in the strength of the Lord, who directed my way for good; and I feared nothing till I arrived at the ship. And on that same day on which I arrived, the ship moved out of its place.[2]

Patrick eventually found his way to his parents in Britain, intending to spend the rest of his life there. But Patrick's extraordinary encounters had only begun. A few years later, in A.D. 432, he saw another vision in his sleep:

> There I saw, indeed, in the bosom of the night, a man coming as it were from Ireland, Victoricus by name, with innumerable letters, and he gave one of them to me. And I read the beginning of the letter containing "The voice of the Irish." And while I was reading aloud the beginning of the letters, I myself thought indeed in my mind that I heard the voice of those who were near the wood of Foclut, which is close by the Western Sea. And they cried out thus as if with one voice, "We entreat thee, holy youth, that thou come, and henceforth walk among us." And I was deeply moved in heart, and could read no further; and so I awoke.[3]

Patrick followed his destiny and returned to Ireland as a missionary. He worked zealously in various parts of the island for the rest of his life. He founded more than three hundred churches and baptized more than 120,000 persons. His labors were so successful that he came to be known as one who "found Ireland all heathen and left it all Christian."[4]

Giovanni Francesco Bernardone
FRANCIS OF ASSISI
A.D. 1206

Giovanni Bernardone was the son of Peter Bernardone, a wealthy Italian textile merchant. His mother was from a distinguished French family. He was baptized as "John," but his parents' love for France prompted them to call him Francis.

Francis' jovial disposition, along with his father's wealth, made him a leader among the young men of Assisi. He was, above all, an elaborate dresser. Francis developed a love for France. Hearing the stories of Arthur and Charlemagne, he was taken captive by the imagination of knights and Gothic chivalry.

Francis' life was interrupted when he was taken captive in a battle with a neighboring city. He was taken to Perugia, where he was kept in prison for two years. While in prison Francis would declare to his prison companions, "I shall be a great man!" Francis returned home with ambitions of following Count Gentile da Fabriano and being knighted by him. He prepared for his journey by outfitting himself with all the magnificent dress and elaborate equipment of a full-fledged knight. But before his departure Francis met a certain knight who, though evidently of noble birth, was unable to conceal his dire poverty. Since true knights were to do good deeds, Francis generously

43

gave this knight all his elaborate armor and expensive apparel.

That very evening Francis had a dream. In his dream a voice called him by name and led him into a room containing an enormous array of weapons of war and military equipment. Francis, having just given away all his armor, asked to whom the armor belonged, and to his surprise, the voice said that it all belonged to him. Encouraged by this dream, Francis left the following morning in search of the honors of knighthood and chivalry for which he was surely destined.

Francis set out on his journey, and when he reached Spoleto, he had another dream. This time the voice was asking him where he was going. Without hesitation he answered that he was going to Apulia to get his knighthood. The voice then said, "Which is better to serve, the master or the servant?" Francis replied, "The master, of course." Then the voice answered: "Then why do you serve the servant instead of the master, the poor instead of the rich?" Then Francis knew who was speaking. "Lord," he said, "what do you want me to do?"

"Go home," the voice answered. "There you will be told what to do."[1]

His friends welcomed Francis home but soon realized that he had changed. The luxury he had enjoyed and had at times paraded before their eyes no longer had an attraction for Francis. In fact, he saw it as a hindrance between him and his fellow man.[2]

Tired of waiting for his guidance from the Lord, Francis set out for Rome to visit the tombs of the apostles. Seeing how many poor beggars there were and how small were the offerings of the other pilgrims, Francis flung his purseful of money through the open grating, which made such a noise that everyone took notice.[3] He exchanged clothes with a beggar and sat all day at St. Peter's tomb begging for alms in perfect French. From that day on, Francis identified himself with the poor.

After returning to Assisi, Francis again heard the voice:

Francis, you must now learn to despise and hate what you have hitherto loved in the flesh, if you will understand my will. And once you have begun to do this, you will find that all that was bitter and hard becomes sweet and pleasant, and all that you thought of with terror and gloom will bring you happiness and peace.[4]

Encountering a leper one day, Francis, who had always been repulsed by people with disfigurements, allowed himself to be embraced and kissed by the leper. In his last will and testament Francis noted that he had since then found joy in the company of lepers and in caring for them, for in the sick and the poor he had learned to recognize the Lord.[5]

When Francis sold some of the fine cloth from his father's warehouse and gave it away, it added fuel to the conflict over his generosity that had been smoldering for some time. His father probably determined at about this time to renounce or disown Francis. Before he could do so, Francis, standing before the court of Bishop Guido, said, "My lord, I will gladly give back to him [his father] not only his money, but all my clothes which I have had from him." While Francis' words were still in the ears of everyone present, he stripped himself naked and laid the clothes before his father.

The renunciation of all worldly things was the decisive act committing Francis to a life of service. He was like the man in the biblical parable who had found a pearl of great price and had sold everything he had to obtain it.

A group of dedicated disciples joined themselves together to follow the teaching and example of Francis. They were called the Friars Minor (the Lesser Brothers) and were approved by Pope Innocent III as an official order of the church in 1209. Today they are simply known as Franciscans.

Thomas Aquinas
SCHOLAR AND THEOLOGIAN
DECEMBER 6, 1273

Thomas Aquinas, the greatest scholastic theologian of the Middle Ages, was born in 1225 into a noble Italian family. In order that he might receive the best education available, Thomas' family sent him at the age of five to study at a nearby monastery. At age fourteen he was enrolled at the University of Naples. Thomas learned his lessons well—too well, however, for his parents' liking. He was so impressed by his Dominican instructor that he decided to become a monk. His parents were horrified at the idea, and tried desperately to dissuade their idealistic and misguided son.

Eventually, they tried to tempt him with a prostitute, thinking that such a moral failure would cause him to give up on his plans to be a monk. When that didn't work, his father attempted to buy for his son the more respectable position of Archbishop of Naples. None of these endeavors were successful. Thomas became a Dominican, and set off to study at the University of Paris. As a last resort, his parents sent men to kidnap him on his way to Paris. But Thomas never would give in, and eventually he was released to go to Paris.

Young Thomas was nicknamed "Dumb Ox" because he was heavy and slow. He was, however, anything but dumb. He was a brilliant scholar who spent his whole life teaching and writing.

The Middle Ages had seen a revival of interest in the classical philosophers. Practically all of Christian theology written before Aquinas was based on, or was similar to, Platonic or Neoplatonic philosophy. Aristotle, in contrast to Plato, was the materialist of the ancient world, believing that the only way to reliable knowledge was through the five senses and through the application of reason to the evidence of the senses. Consequently, spiritual experiences were disqualified as unreliable knowledge. For this reason, most in the church saw the teachings of Aristotle as a challenge to Christianity.[1]

That, in fact, is what made Thomas Aquinas so controversial. Thomas based the whole of his system of thought on Aristotelian philosophy. This constituted a break with the teaching of church fathers who, for the first twelve centuries of the church, based their worldview on revelation, not on reason.

Thomas Aquinas' great contribution was that, by assimilating the philosophy of Aristotle, he articulated a faith in Christianity that was based on reason. That made it more palatable to the secular mind and provided a basis for the logical defense of the faith. However, the emphasis on logic, reason, and Aristotelian materialism left little or no room for knowledge based on revelation or on mystical experiences.[2]

Thomas' writings fill eighteen large volumes. His most important work, *Summa Theologiae*, was never finished—because of a divine encounter that has always been a mystery to students of Aquinas. On December 6, 1273, while celebrating Mass in the chapel of Saint Nicholas, Thomas himself had a supernatural vision, after which he stopped his writing forever. When his friend Reginald asked him to return to his normal habit of reading, writing, and engaging in the latest controversies, Thomas said emphatically, "I can write no more!" After some time had passed Reginald again reminded Thomas of his need to finish *Summa Theologiae*. Thomas answered with even greater firmness, "I can write no more. I have seen things which make all my writings like straw."[3]

It is impossible to know exactly what Thomas meant by that statement. It is, perhaps, a reference to the fact that his logical approach was an inadequate way of understanding his relationship with God.

Thomas Aquinas never worked again on *Summa Theologiae*. He died on March 7 of the following year, at the age of forty-nine.

TEN

Jeanne La Pucelle

JOAN OF ARC

1425-1431

*J*eanne la Pucelle was born in 1412 on the Feast of Epiphany in the village of Domremy, France. Her father, Jacques d' Arc, was a peasant farmer, a man well respected and of standing in the local community. Though she never learned to read or write, Joan mastered the arts of sewing and spinning.

Much of the information about Joan comes from an investigation done by the church only a few years after her death. In those inquiries the local priest and Joan's former playmates recalled her love for prayer and for the church, her care for the sick, and her sympathy for wayfarers, to whom she often gave up her own bed.

What would have been a happy childhood for Joan was overshadowed by the political upheavals and military conflicts that dominated the fifteenth century. Mark Twain once said, "[Joan's] century was the brutalest, the wickedest, the rottenest in history since the Dark Ages." France had been at war with England off and on for decades in what is now called the Hundred Years War. Joan was only a child when King Henry V of England invaded France and claimed the French crown of the insane King Charles VI.

France itself had fallen into a civil war, led by the Duke of Burgundy in northern France and the Duke of Orleans in the south. Consequently, there was no unified resistance against the English, and King Henry V captured all of Normandy. The Burgundians joined forces with the English and supported Henry V's claim to the throne. These famous lines from Shakespeare refer to Henry V's defeat of the French at the Battle of Agincourt (from, of course, an English perspective):

> We few, we happy few, we band of brothers.
> For he today that sheds his blood with me
> Shall be my brother; be he ne'er so vile [lowly],
> This day shall gentle his condition [raise to the rank of gentlemen].
> And gentlemen in England now abed [men who stayed at home]
> Shall think themselves accursed they were not here,
> And hold their manhoods cheap whiles any speaks
> That fought with us upon Saint Crispin's Day.[1]
>
> Shakespeare's *Henry V*

In 1422, when Joan was only ten, King Henry and crazy King Charles both died. That, however, did not put an end to the conflict. The Duke of Bedford, regent for the infant King of England, continued to pursue the war and the claim to the French throne. The English and their Burgundian allies captured one fortified town after another. Charles VII, heir (or "dauphin") to the throne of his father, was unusually ugly, physically weak, and a complete coward. He considered the situation hopeless and spent most of his time in frivolous pastimes with his court.

There was great fear throughout the parts of France not yet under the rule of the English. The future of France looked hopeless. Their enemies were united and, had Charles VII the heart to save his own kingdom, who would have rallied to him as a leader?

In 1425, when Joan was fourteen years old, she had her first divine encounter. She had been dancing in her father's garden along with several of her girlfriends. Joan sat down under a tree to rest. Suddenly, she saw a great light and heard a voice speak to her.

For a long time she told no one about what she had seen and heard, fearing what others might think. But again and again she continued to hear the voice. At first she was only encouraged to be faithful to God. But by May 1428 the voice had become more specific in its instructions. She had been chosen by God, she was told, to go and rescue France from invaders and to insure that the dauphin was crowned king of France.

The frightened peasant girl cried out, "I am but a poor maid and know nothing of war." The voice merely answered, "God will help you."[2]

Joan at first did nothing. But the voice kept coming to her, "Daughter of God, go, go, go. I will come to your aid."[3] Finally Joan persuaded her uncle to take her to the nearby town of Vaucouleurs to present herself to the commander of the King's forces. On the first visit she was rejected and returned home. But in January 1429 she went to the commander again. The voice had specifically told her she was to lead an army that would relieve the siege of Orleans. Again she was rejected, but this time she was determined and would not return home. The longer she hung around the more the word spread everywhere of the young peasant girl who wanted to save France. Eventually, it was even heard by Charles VII, and Joan was summoned to his royal castle in Chinton.

Dressed as a man, she traveled with three soldiers for eleven days through Burgundian territory. The soldiers were amazed at the feisty young girl who had the courage of a soldier yet insisted on going to Mass, even in enemy territory.

Joan traveled 350 miles and arrived in Chinton on February 24, 1429. On the following evening she was summoned to the king's court. More than three hundred people had assembled for the event. Joan is said to have proceeded directly to Charles VII, who had disguised himself among those in attendance. The contrast between Joan and the dauphin was dramatic. Joan, a peasant girl dressed in simple male clothes, exuded confidence and conviction. The dauphin, dressed in royal attire, was a weak, indecisive man, afraid to even cross a bridge if perchance it might fall while he was on it.

Joan's confidence made an impression on the dauphin, who took her aside for a private meeting in which he further questioned her. It is uncertain what took place in that meeting, but the dauphin emerged with quite a changed expression. All present agreed he looked as if he had seen an angel. What is certain is that Joan repeated to the dauphin that she should be given an army immediately. The voice had told her that her time was short. "I will last but a year—scarcely more," she said.

As impressed as Charles VII was, his advisors were skeptical, and he was too weak-willed to overrule them. To settle the matter Joan was sent to the city of Poitiers to be examined by a learned group of theologians there. The questioning went on for several weeks. Though Joan could neither read nor write, her simple, candid answers revealed the pettiness and unbelief of the theologians. When asked if she believed in God, Joan responded, "More than you do." When asked to show a sign, she said, "I have not come to Poitiers to make signs. Take me to Orleans, and I will show you the signs for which I have been sent!" Then she went on to explain in detail the signs the voice said would be given at Orleans. Joan promised to end the siege of Orleans (now a lost cause), see that the dauphin was crowned at Rheims, and drive the English out of France.[4] As hard as they had tried, the theologians could find no ground to discredit Joan, and recommended to Charles VII that he make use of her services.

Joan began to prepare the troops. She forbade the men to swear, or to pillage on the march to Orleans, and insisted that the prostitutes lingering around the camp be driven away. Upon their arrival at Orleans, Joan's commanders were reluctant. The English had built seven forts around the city, and the commanders wanted to wait. Their goal was merely to deliver supplies and cheer up the people of Orleans. "The advice of our Lord is wiser and more certain than yours," Joan warned them.

On April 29, 1429, the army of Charles VII, led by Joan of Arc, clad in white armor, entered the city of Orleans. The commanders inside were also distrustful and reluctant to engage the superior English forces in a direct assault. But the voice was continuing to insist that Joan press ahead because God was with them and had granted them victory. Under the determined and courageous leadership of a teenage peasant girl, and against any reasonable probability of success, the French captured all the English forts surrounding Orleans.

Upon Joan's insistence, and over the objection of those who wanted to negotiate with the English, Charles VII was crowned king of France in Rheims. This event completed the mission entrusted to Joan by the voice. It also marked the end of Joan's miraculous military successes against overwhelming odds. As the voice had said, her time was short. Joan led an attack on Paris which failed, mainly for lack of the support promised by King Charles. Indeed the king, fearing her popularity, had intentionally betrayed Joan.

Joan was sent to assist the city of Compiegne, which was being attacked by Burgundian forces. On the way she was told by the voice that she would be captured before St. John's Day (June 24). She arrived at Compiegne on May 22 and on the next day led an attack against the enemy siege. But the mercenary forces that had been sent with her retreated into the city and the drawbridge was raised, leaving Joan vulnerable. She was captured and held prisoner by the Duke of Burgundy. It was customary in those times that any prisoner of high rank be held for ransom. But despite an outpouring of sympathy from the French people, Charles VII made no effort on Joan's behalf. Eventually, the Duke of Burgundy sold Joan to the English.

Joan's execution was a foregone conclusion, but the English could not condemn her to death for defeating them in open warfare. They could, however, have her condemned as a sorceress and heretic. The English and the Burgundians had already concluded that only by sorcery could they have been defeated. During the course of six public and nine private sessions before the ecclesiastical court, Joan was examined and cross-examined incessantly for hour after hour regarding her visions and the voices. Pierre Cauchon was the chief inquisitor. His questions, and Joan's answers, included the following:

Cauchon: "Was it God's will that you should come to France?"

Joan: "I had rather have been torn in pieces by four horses than have come to France for any other reason."

Cauchon: "Do you believe in your voices?"

Joan: "I believe in them as I believe in God, and as I believe that Our Lord Jesus Christ suffered in His Death and Passion."

Cauchon: "Do they speak to you often?"

Joan: "They are speaking to me here, in this very place. They say, 'Answer boldly; be of good heart; God will help you.'"[5]

Joan answered all the inquisitors' questions, except those which had to do with the divine revelations she had declared to the dauphin. Joan persistently refused to reveal those secrets:

Cauchon: "Of what kind were the revelations made to the King?"

Joan: "Send a messenger to him, and he will tell you."

Cauchon: "Is it unpleasing to God that you should speak the truth?"

Joan: "No, but it is His pleasure that I should tell to the King what concerns the King, and not to you."[6]

The inquisitor pressed on in his efforts to entrap Joan, and at one point she declared to him what the voices had assured her about the inevitable defeat of the English:

Cauchon: "Have you not conceived a lively animosity against the Burgundians?"

Joan: "My only feeling is a firm determination to set the King again in his Kingdom."

Cauchon: "Does God hate the English?"

Joan: "I know nothing of any love or hatred which God may bear to the English; but I do know that God will give to Frenchmen the victory against them."

Cauchon: "Was God, then, for the English, when they were winning?"

Joan: "That I do not know, but only that if they are beaten it will be because of their sins. Before seven years have passed the English will suffer a far worse setback than they did at Orleans, and will lose a far greater stake…. The King shall be reestablished in his Kingdom, whether his enemies wish it or no. I know that as surely as I know that you are sitting there before me. I say this now so that when what I tell you shall have come to pass, men may remember my words. I know for a certainty that the English will all be driven out of France; all, that is, except those who shall die here."[7]

Joan's shrewd answers, produced without the aid of an advocate, astonished and often embarrassed her prosecutors. Nevertheless, she was condemned and handed over to secular authorities to be executed if she did not recant.

Joan refused to deny the visions or the voices, even upon the threat of torture. Joan was terrified at the prospect of being burned, and at one point, when the sentence was being read condemning her to being burned at the stake, she did weaken and make some sort of retraction. But a short time later, after being returned to her prison cell, Joan regained her courage and reaffirmed that God had truly sent her and that her voices came from God.

On May 29, 1431, Joan, not yet twenty years old, was burned at the stake as a relapsed heretic.

Joan's death had a profound effect on all who witnessed it. John Tressart, one of the King's secretaries, exclaimed, "We are lost: we have burned a saint!"[8] Even Charles VII, the despicable king, was affected by the news. The contrasts between Joan and Charles were dramatic. On the one hand was the peasant girl who exuded courage, determination, and integrity. On the other was the king who lived a life of extravagance and unbridled self-indulgence and was filled with fearfulness, uncertainty, and deceit. The French king had actually conspired with both the English and the church to betray Joan. Afterward, due in large part to Joan's influence, it was Charles VII who "recanted" his ways. He changed his indulgent lifestyle and actually became a serious, hard-working monarch. He even chose some of Joan's knights as his advisors. Eventually, the English were completely routed from France, fulfilling Joan's vision.

ELEVEN

Christopher Columbus
MAPMAKER AND EXPLORER
1491, 1502

Christopher Columbus was an expert navigator, a skilled map-maker, and a visionary. He was also a devout Christian, though his religious devotion saw many ups and down. In the early days his stumbling block was rejection and discouragement; later in life, it was the lust for gold, power, and fame. As a young man Columbus devoured the Scriptures and even wrote a commentary entitled *Book of Prophecies*. Available only in Spanish, it is largely a compilation of all the teachings and prophecies in the Bible on the subjects of the earth, distant lands, population movements, and undiscovered tribes.

When Columbus appealed for today's equivalent of half a million dollars to fund his explorations, he was rejected by King John II of Portugal, then by Henry VII of England and Ferdinand and Isabella of Spain. He was discouraged and despondent, but nevertheless claimed that his plan had been given him by divine revelation:

> It was the Lord who put into my mind—I could feel His hand upon me—the fact that it would be possible to sail from here to the Indies.... All who heard of my project rejected it with laughter, ridiculing me.... There is no question that the inspiration was from the Holy Spirit, because He comforted me with rays of marvelous

illumination from the Holy Scriptures.... For the execution of the journey to the Indies I did not make use of intelligence, mathematics, or maps. It is simply the fulfillment of what Isaiah had prophesied.... No one should fear to undertake any task in the name of our Savior, if it is just and if the intention is purely for His Holy service... the fact that the Gospel must still be preached to so many lands in such a short time—this is what convinces me.[1]

King Ferdinand and Queen Isabella finally granted Columbus the funding for his expedition. He set sail in 1492 and landed in what he thought was the East Indies. Unknowingly, he had discovered North America.

Numerous expeditions would follow in Columbus' wake, most of them in search of gold. Columbus himself made several other voyages to North America. Having begun with the purpose of advancing the kingdom of God, he too in his later years was consumed by the lust for gold and by the desire to be properly honored for his discovery.

In 1502, on his fourth and last voyage to the New World, Columbus sailed southward down the coast of Central America and finally found the gold with which he had become so intoxicated. But at what a price! Columbus had sailed up into a river, and having sent out parties to gather water and provisions, he was all but left alone on the ship. He then heard shouts and shooting, and then there was silence.

That evening, when the tide was going out, Columbus began to see the bodies of several of his men floating down the river. In his journal Columbus recorded on this occasion another divine encounter, one in which he was rebuked for what he had done with the opportunities given to him:[2]

I toiled up to the highest point of the ship, calling in a trembling voice with fast-falling fear to the war captains at every point of the compass, but never did they answer me. Exhausted, I fell asleep, groaning. I heard a very compassionate voice, saying "O fool and slow to believe and to serve thy God, the God of all!... Since thou wast born, ever has He had thee in His most watchful care.... The Indies, which are so rich a part of the world, He gave thee for thine own; thou hast divided them as it pleased thee.... Of the barriers of the Ocean Sea, which were closed with such mighty chains, He gave thee the keys....What did He more for the people of Israel when He brought them out of Egypt? Or for David, whom from a shepherd He made to be king in Judea? Turn thyself to Him, and acknowledge thine error; His mercy is infinite...."

I heard all this as if I were in a trance, but I had no answer to give to words so true, but could only weep for my errors. He, who-ever he was who spoke to me, ended saying, "Fear not; have trust; all these tribulations are written upon marble and are not without cause."[3]

Through sickness, storms, and many perilous setbacks, Columbus and the remainder of his crew finally made it back to Spain. In his last days, however, he returned to his longtime obsession of trying to secure the rights and honor that belonged to him as the discoverer of the New World. All of his requests to King Ferdinand were answered by more stalling and empty promises. On Ascension Day, 1506, after receiving the sacraments of the church, and having said, "Father, into Thy hands I commend my spirit," Columbus died.[4]

TWELVE

Blaise Pascal
SCIENTIST AND MATHEMATICIAN
NOVEMBER 23, 1654

*I*n 1626, when Blaise Pascal was only three, his mother died, leaving his father, Etienne Pascal, to care for Blaise, Gilberte, and their baby sister Jacqueline. When Blaise was eight, his father "sold his position" as a judge and devoted himself entirely to his son's education. The young Pascal was taught to think for himself, stimulated by observations, questions, and conversation with his father. Only after mastering Latin and Greek would he be allowed to study geometry. However, Blaise's curiosity could not be checked. At the age of twelve he began to study geometry on his own, and before his father knew what he was doing, Pascal is said to have arrived at the equivalent of Euclid's first thirty-two theorems.[1]

The Pascal family was dutifully religious, but religion did not seem to have any personal effect on them; none, that is, until 1646, when an accidental slip on the ice left Etienne with a broken leg. Etienne sent for the de la Bouteillerie brothers, famous bonesetters who had been converted to Jansenism, a movement based on Augustine's theology of grace, and who were now devoting themselves to charitable work. During the three months these two medical missionaries lived in the Pascal household, they talked about having a personal experience with God.

These admirable representatives of Christ provided many books for the Pascal family. Eventually, Blaise was converted, at least intellectually, and soon converted his whole family as well. His father, Jacqueline, Gilberte and her husband all became dedicated Christians as a result of Blaise's fiery zeal.

Shortly after his "intellectual conversion," Pascal published his paper on the principles of vacuum, which led to his experiments in hydrodynamics. He also invented the first working calculator. But having buried himself in his experiments, he withdrew from the company of the saints and was again seduced by the ways of the world.

By 1653 the twenty-nine-year-old genius had fallen into a deep depression. Jacqueline wrote that he was seized by "a great scorn of the world and an unbearable disgust for all the people who are in it."[2] His cheerful confidence in grace had vanished. Most of all, he was amazed and horrified at his own apathy. "It is a horrible thing," Pascal wrote, "to feel everything one possesses slip away."[3]

In September of 1654, Jacqueline wrote to her sister, Gilberte, concerning a visit from their brother: "On this visit he opened himself to me in a pitiful way, admitting to me that in the midst of his occupations, which were great … he found himself detached from all things in a way that he had never been before…that also he was in such a great abandonment on God's part that he felt no attraction in that direction."[4]

On November 23, 1654, Blaise Pascal experienced what is known as his "second conversion," the first being of the intellect and the second of the heart. Pascal recorded that from 10:30 in the evening until 12:30 A.M., he had a divine encounter with the "God of Abraham,

God of Isaac, God of Jacob, not of the philosophers and scholars." He also said that he then made the following resolve: "Total submission to Jesus Christ and to my director."[5]

Two years later, after his niece (Gilberte's daughter) was miraculously healed of a growth the size of a hazelnut in the corner of her eye, Pascal began collecting material for a work he planned to call *Apology for the Christian Religion*. The book was never written. All that remains today are his notes. Pascal, who had given all of his possessions to the poor, in 1662 gave shelter to a poor family who eventually contracted smallpox. Rather than evict them, Pascal moved in with Gilberte. He became ill and died on August 19, 1662, at the age of thirty-nine.

A few days after Pascal's death, a servant noticed a curious bulge sewn into his jacket. He pulled out a parchment written in Pascal's own hand, along with a second piece of paper on which the words were copied with a few additions. The parchment seems to have been notes taken during or just after Pascal's two-hour divine encounter. For eight years he had carried the paper, wearing it as a secret amulet next to his heart. The original parchment has disappeared, but a copy was made by Pascal's nephew, and Pascal's own copy—the one found in the jacket—remains as one of the treasures of the Bibliotheque Nationale in Paris. At the top of the sheet of paper stands a cross. Below are the following notes:

Monday, 23 November, day of Saint Clement, pope and martyr, and of others in the martyrology.
Eve of Saint Chrysogonus, martyr and others,

From about half past ten in the evening until about half past twelve,

..... FIRE .....

God of Abraham, God of Isaac, God of Jacob, not of the philosophers and scholars.

Certitude, certitude, feeling, joy, peace.

God of Jesus Christ.

Deum meun et Deum vestrum [My God and your God].

Thy God will be my God.

Forgetfulness of the world and of everything, except GOD.

He is to be found only by the ways taught in the Gospel.

Greatness of the human soul.

O righteous Father, the world has not known thee, but I have known thee.

Joy, joy, joy, tears of joy.

I have been separated from him.

Dereliquerunt me fontem aquae vivae [They have forsaken me, the fountains of living waters].

My God, wilt thou forsake me?

Let me not be separated from him eternally.

This is the eternal life, that they know thee as the only true God, and the one whom thou hast sent, Jesus Christ.

Jesus Christ,

Jesus Christ.

I have been separated from him; I have fled him, renounced him, crucified him,

Let me never be separated from him.

He is preserved only by the ways taught in the Gospel.
Renunciation, total and sweet.

The copy of the original made by Pascal's nephew ends here. Pascal's copy added the lines:

Total submission to Jesus Christ and to my director.
Eternally in joy for a day's trial on earth.
Non obliviscar sermones tuos [I will not forget Thy Word]. Amen.[6]

John Wesley
FOUNDER OF THE METHODIST CHURCH
MAY 24, 1738

*J*ohn Wesley is said to have "saved England" from moral and social collapse. Wesley, a minister of the Anglican Church, was a missionary to Georgia for a brief time, after which he returned to England discouraged and uncertain of his own standing with God. On May 24, 1738, in a meetinghouse on Aldersgate Street in London, Wesley listened to the reading of Martin Luther's *Preface to Romans.* In his reflection on his experience that evening, Wesley wrote in his familiar style of understatement that his heart was "strangely warmed." One historian has written, "What happened in that little room was of more importance to England than all the victories of Pitt by land or sea."[1]

Wesley was convinced that at all cost the people of Britain must hear the good news of salvation. He preached wherever people would listen, before dawn to coal miners going to work and even from atop his father's tombstone. He traveled more than 250,000 miles on horseback, preached 40,000 sermons, wrote hundreds of books and pamphlets, and pioneered a monthly magazine. His original intention was to reform the Anglican Church, but reluctantly he became the founder of the Methodist Church.

On New Year's Day 1739, a remarkable "love feast" was held at Fetter Lane in London. John and Charles Wesley were present, along with George Whitefield. John Wesley recorded in his journal:

About three in the morning, as we were continuing instant in prayer the power of God came mightily upon us insomuch that many cried out for exceeding joy and many fell to the ground. As soon as we were recovered a little from that awe and amazement at the presence of His majesty, we broke out with one voice, "We praise Thee, O God, we acknowledge Thee to be the Lord!"[2]

This New Year's Pentecost confirmed that Wesley and his friends were in the early days of a great spiritual renewal. In the years that followed, the "English Awakening," fueled by the preaching of John Wesley, transformed all of England. George Whitefield went to preach in the American Colonies, beginning what has come to be known as the "First Great Awakening."

On March 17, 1746 Wesley recorded in his journal another strange occurrence:

I left Newcastle and set out with Mr. Downes and Mr. Shepherd. But when we came to Smeton, Mr. Downes was so ill that he could go no further. When Mr. Shepherd and I left Smeton, my horse was so lame that I was afraid I would have to leave it behind as well. We could not discern what it was that was wrong; and yet he would scarcely put his foot to the ground. By riding this way for seven miles, I was thoroughly tired, and my head ached more than it had for some months. (What I say here is the naked fact: let every man account for it as he sees good.) I then thought, "Cannot God heal either man or beast, by any means, or without any?" Immediately my weariness and headache ceased, and my horse's lameness in the same instant. Nor did he halt any more either that day or the next. A very odd accident this also![3]

On October 15, 1770, Whitefield died as he always hoped he would—in the midst of a preaching tour—in Newport, Rhode Island. Charles Wesley died in 1788 and John in 1791. They are jointly commemorated on a wall medallion in Westminster Abbey with the inscription, "The best of all, God is with us."

FOURTEEN

George Frideric Handel

COMPOSER OF *MESSIAH*
SEPTEMBER 15, 1741

*O*n Saturday, August 22, 1741, George Frideric Handel, the German-born composer, sat down at his desk in the front room of his house in London. After bowing his head to ask the Lord's blessing, he wrote at the top of a blank piece of paper, "Messiah."

His quill pen could hardly keep up with the musical notes and harmonies that soon began to flow through his mind. Hour by hour and day by day he wrote. He continued morning, noon, and night. All food placed at his door by servants remained untouched. He finished the first part in seven days, the second part in nine days, and the final part in six days.

On September 15, twenty-four days after he began, Handel put the final touches on the closing lines of the Hallelujah Chorus. Emerging from his study with tears streaming down his face, he cried out to the startled servant who met him, *"I did tink I did see all heffen before me, und da great Gott himself!"*

George Washington
CAPTAIN, VIRGINIA MILITIA
JULY 7, 1755

*Y*oung George Washington received a letter from General Edward Braddock's headquarters in Alexandria, Virginia, inviting him to serve as an aide to the General. Washington knew the wilderness, and Braddock, commander of the British forces in the American colonies, needed his expertise. The objective was to march a combined force of Virginia Militia and well-trained British Redcoats through the wilderness to capture Fort Duquesne, the French stronghold located where the Allegheny and Monongahela Rivers join together to form the Ohio River. It is today downtown Pittsburgh, the site of Duquesne University and Three Rivers Stadium.

No one in Virginia had ever seen such an army as the one assembling in northern Virginia. These were disciplined British troops. With their red coats, brass buttons, and polished rifles, supported by the finest artillery on the continent, they appeared invincible.

Soon Washington discovered that what an old friend, Lord Fairfax, told him about Braddock was true: "He is a stranger to both fear and common sense, and his best fitness to fight Indians is that he is providentially bald. He is a brave but reckless man."[1]

Benjamin Franklin, however, had warned Braddock of the dangers he faced:

You will be marching through a narrow road through pathless, dense forests. You will be in constant danger of being cut into, for the French and Indians are dexterous in ambuscades. And to send back relief quickly, if attacked, will be nigh impossible, with woods all about you.[2]

Washington had tried to tell Braddock the same thing, but he refused to listen. They would march in lines as the soldiers had been trained. They would kneel in a perfectly straight line and shoot together. To Braddock, hiding behind trees was for cowards and undisciplined troops (like the Virginia Militia).

The British had cut a road through the dense wilderness and on July 7, 1755, had come to within twelve miles of Fort Duquesne. The line of two thousand Redcoats marched in strict military order with drums beating and the Union Jack flapping in the wind. Braddock assured his officers that they would be eating dinner in the fort that evening.

Captain Washington was pleased to hear that Major Thomas Gage and his men had crossed the Monongahela River ford without an ambush. But with a grim face, Christopher Gist, Washington's frontier friend, shook his head and informed Captain Washington that the Indians had been watching them for miles.

Up at the front of the column a single musket fired out of the forest. It was soon followed by heavy firing, blood-curdling war whoops, and then more firing. The road was just twelve feet wide, with walls of dense trees on either side. They were trapped. Men were dying by the hundreds, and in the chaos all those who were able fled back in the direction from which they had come.

General Braddock, Captain Washington, and other officers rode toward the front of the column and attempted to turn them back, but it was a stampede. "It was," said Washington, "as if we had tried to stop the wild bears of the mountains." All military order was gone, and those who were stampeding in retreat down the narrow corridor ran headlong into those trying to advance. All the while, musket balls were whistling through the air in every direction.

The Indians then turned their guns on the officers, who sat high on their horses above the confusion. One by one they fell. Washington's horse was hit and fell dead under him. He grabbed a riderless horse and leaped on it. Looking around at the confusion and carnage, Captain Washington realized that he was the only officer left. Said one who had his eye on Washington, "I expected every moment to see him fall. Nothing but the superintending care of Providence could have saved him."[3]

A group of Virginians ducked behind trees to provide cover as Washington ordered retreat through the wilderness. The Monongahela River was red with the blood of wounded, retreating soldiers.[4]

Afterwards, Washington reflected on the battle in a letter to his brother, Jack, who had come to manage the Mount Vernon plantation in George's absence.

As I have heard, since my arrival at this place, a circumstantial account of my death and dying speech, I take this opportunity of contradicting the first, and of assuring you, that I have not as yet composed the latter. But, by the all-powerful dispensation of Providence, I have been protected beyond all human probability of expectation; for I have four bullets through my coat, and two horses shot under me, yet escaped unhurt, although death was leveling my companions on every side of me![5]

Fifteen years after the Battle of Monongahela, George Washington and his lifelong friend, Dr. James Craik, were exploring the wilderness territory in the Western Reserve. Craik had been with him at Monongahela, and was wounded there. Near the place where the Ohio and the Kanawha Rivers join, they met up with a group of Indians who had been searching for them. The leader was an old chief who sought to speak to Washington. A council fire was built, and the chief relayed these words through an interpreter:

I am a chief and ruler over my tribes. My influence extends to the waters of the great lakes, and to the far blue mountains. I have traveled a long and weary path, that I might see the young warrior of the great battle. It was on the day when the white man's blood mixed with the streams of our forest, that I first beheld this chief. I called to my young men and said, "Mark yon tall and daring warrior? He is not of the red-coat tribe—he hath an Indian's wisdom, and his warriors fight as we do—himself alone is exposed. Quick, let your aim be certain, and he dies." Our rifles were leveled, rifles which, but for him, knew not how to miss....'Twas all in vain; a power mightier far than we shielded him from harm. He cannot die in battle. I am old, and soon shall be gathered to the great council fire of my fathers in the land of shades, but ere I go, there is something that bids me speak in the voice of prophecy: Listen! The Great Spirit protects that man, and guides his destinies—he will become the chief of nations, and a people yet unborn will hail him as the founder of a mighty empire.[6]

George Washington
COMMANDER OF THE CONTINENTAL ARMY
WINTER 1777

*W*hile the British General Howe and his army of Redcoats were comfortably boarded in warm Philadelphia homes, Washington and the Continental Army camped fifteen miles away at Valley Forge. Washington describes the grim condition in that winter of 1777:

> No history now extant can furnish an instant of an army's suffering such uncommon hardships as ours has done and bearing them with the same patience and fortitude. To see men without clothes to cover their nakedness, without blankets to lie on, without shoes (for the want of which their marches might be traced by the blood from their feet)....[1]
>
> I am now convinced beyond a doubt that this army must inevitably be reduced to one or the other of these three things: starve, dissolve, or disperse in order to obtain subsistence.[2]

Historians generally credit Washington as having achieved his greatest feat in holding the Continental Army together through the winter at Valley Forge.

Anthony Sherman, at age eighteen, was a firsthand observer at Valley Forge. In 1859, before he died, Sherman related to his friend Wesley Braushaw his recollections of his close association with George

Washington. What follows is Braushaw's record of Sherman's account, as published in the December 1880 edition of *The National Tribune*:

The last time I ever saw Anthony Sherman was on the 4th of July, 1859, in Independence Square. He was then ninety-nine years old, and becoming very feeble; but though so old, his dimming eye rekindled as he gazed upon Independence Hall, which he had come to gaze upon once more before he was gathered home. "Let's go to the Hall," he said. "I want to tell you an incident of Washington's life—one which no one alive knows of except myself....

"From the beginning of the Revolution we experienced all phases of fortune—now good and now ill, one time victorious and another conquered. The darkest period we had, I think, was when Washington, after several reverses, retreated to Valley Forge, where he resolved to pass the Winter of '77....

"You have doubtless heard the story of Washington going to the thicket to pray. Well, it was not only true, but he used often to pray in secret for aid and comfort from God, the interposition of whose Divine Providence brought us safely through those days of tribulation.

"One day, I remember it well, when the chilly winds whistled through the leafless trees, though the sky was cloudless and the sun shone brightly, he [Washington] remained in his quarters nearly all the afternoon alone. When he came out, I noticed that his face was a shade paler than usual. There seemed to be something on his mind of more than ordinary importance. Returning just after dusk, he dispatched an orderly to the quarters who was presently in attendance. After a preliminary conversation of about an hour, Washington, gazing upon his companion with that strange look of dignity which he alone commanded, said to the latter: 'I do not know whether it is owing to the anxiety of my mind or what, but this afternoon as I was sitting at this very table engaged in preparing a dispatch, something seemed to disturb me. Looking up, I beheld standing opposite me a singularly beautiful female. So astonished was I, for I had given strict orders not to be disturbed, that it was some moments before I found language to inquire the cause of her presence. A second, a third, and even a fourth time did I repeat my question, but received no answer from my mysterious visitor except a slight raising of her eyes.

"'By this time I felt strange sensations spreading through me. I would have risen but the riveted gaze of the being before me rendered volition impossible. I assayed once more to address her, but my tongue had become useless, as though it had become paralyzed.

"'A new influence, mysterious, potent, irresistible, took possession of me. All I could do was to gaze steadily, vacantly at my unknown visitor. Gradually the surrounding atmosphere seemed as if it had become filled with sensations, and luminous. Everything about me seemed to rarify, the mysterious visitor herself becoming more airy and yet more distinct to my sight than before. I now began to feel as one dying, or rather to experience the sensations which I have sometimes imagined accompany dissolution. I did not think, I did not reason, I did not move; all were alike impossible. I was only conscious of gazing fixedly, vacantly at my companion.

"'Presently I heard a voice saying, "Son of the Republic, look and learn," while at the same time my visitor extended her arm eastwardly. I now beheld a heavy white vapor at some distance rising fold upon fold. This gradually dissipated, and I looked upon a strange scene. Before me lay spread out in one vast plain all the countries of the world—Europe, Asia, Africa, and America. I saw rolling and tossing between Europe and America the billows of the Atlantic, and between Asia and America lay the Pacific.

"'"Son of the Republic," said the same mysterious voice as before, "look and learn." At that moment I beheld a dark, shadowy being, like an angel, standing, or rather floating in mid-air, between Europe and America. Dripping water out of the ocean in the hollow of each hand, he sprinkled some upon America with his right hand, while with his left hand he cast some on Europe. Immediately a cloud raised from these countries, and joined in mid-ocean. For a while it remained stationary, and then moved slowly westward, until it enveloped America in its murky folds. Sharp flashes of lightning gleamed through it at intervals, and I heard the smothering groans and cries of the American people.

"'A second time the angel dipped water from the ocean, and sprinkled it out as before. The dark cloud was then drawn back to the ocean, in whose heavy billows it sank from view. A third time I heard the mysterious voice saying, "Son of the Republic, look and learn." I cast my eyes upon America and beheld villages and towns and cities springing up one after another until the whole land from the Atlantic to the Pacific was dotted with them.

"'Again, I heard the mysterious voice say, "Son of the Republic, the end of the century cometh, look and learn." At this the dark shadowy angel turned his face southward, and from Africa I saw an ill-omened specter approach our land. It flitted slowly over every town and city of the latter. The inhabitants presently set themselves in battle array against each other. As I continued looking I saw a bright angel, on whose brow rested a crown of light, on which was traced the word "Union," bearing the American flag which he placed between the divided nation, and said, "Remember ye are brethren." Instantly, the inhabitants, casting from them their weapons, became friends once more, and united around the National Standard.

"'And again I heard the mysterious voice saying, "Son of the Republic, look and learn." At this the dark, shadowy angel placed a trumpet into his mouth, and blew three distinct blasts; and taking water from the ocean, he sprinkled it upon Europe, Asia, and Africa. Then my eyes beheld a fearful scene: from each of these countries arose thick, black clouds that were soon joined into one. Throughout this mass there gleamed a dark red light by which I saw hordes of armed men, who, moving with the cloud, marched by land and sailed by sea to America. Our country was enveloped in the volume of cloud, and I saw these vast armies devastate the whole country and burn the villages, towns, and cities that I beheld springing up. As my ears listened to the thundering of the cannon, clashing of swords, and the shouts and cries of millions in mortal combat, I heard again the mysterious voice saying, "Son of the Republic, look and learn." When the voice had ceased, the dark, shadowy angel placed his trumpet once more to his mouth, and blew a long and fearful blast.

"'Instantly a light as of a thousand suns shone down from above me, and pierced and broke into fragments the dark cloud which enveloped America. At the same moment the angel upon whose head still shone the word Union, and who bore our national flag in one hand and a sword in the other, descended from the heavens attended by legions of white spirits. These immediately joined the inhabitants of America, who I perceived were well nigh overcome, but who, immediately taking courage again, closed up their broken ranks and renewed the battle.

"'Again, amid the fearful noise of the conflict, I heard the mysterious voice saying, "Son of the Republic, look and learn." As the voice ceased, the shadowy angel for the last time dipped water from the ocean and sprinkled it upon America. Instantly the dark cloud rolled back, together with the armies it had brought, leaving the inhabitants of the land victorious!

"'Then once more I beheld the villages, towns, and cities springing up where I had seen them before, while the bright angel, planting the azure standard he had brought in the midst of them, cried with a loud voice: "While the stars remain, and the heavens send down dew upon the earth, so long shall the Union last." And taking from his brow the crown on which blazoned the word "Union," he placed it upon the Standard while the people, kneeling down, said, "Amen."

"'The scene instantly began to fade and dissolve, and I at last saw nothing but the rising, curling vapor I at first beheld. This also disappearing, I found myself once more gazing upon the mysterious visitor, who, in the same voice I had heard before, said,

"Son of the Republic, what you have seen is thus interpreted: Three great perils will come upon the Republic. The most fearful is the third, but in this greatest conflict the whole world united shall not prevail against her. Let every child of the Republic learn to live for his God, his land, and the Union."

"'With these words the vision vanished, and I started from my seat and felt that I had seen a vision wherein had been shown to me the birth, progress, and destiny of the United States. In union she will have her strength, in disunion her destruction.

"Such, my friends," concluded the venerable narrator [Sherman], "were the words I heard from Washington's own lips, and America will do well to profit by them."[3]

There is debate over the authenticity of the account of Washington's Valley Forge vision. Because of the reference to what would be considered the Civil War and the two World Wars of the twentieth century, it sounds to some like an account of a prophecy created after the events it predicted had occurred. However, the earliest published account of the vision predates the Civil War by two years. Whether it was Washington's vision or just a creation of Anthony Sherman's imagination, it accurately predicted the following one hundred years of American history.

SEVENTEEN

Charles Grandison Finney

AMERICA'S GREATEST EVANGELIST
OCTOBER 10, 1821

Charles Finney is often called the father of American revivalism. He was directly responsible for more than five hundred thousand converts in a time when less than ten million people lived in the twenty-four states of the Union. He is one of the most important figures in American history, and it would be impossible to understand the American religious experience without understanding Finney and his influence.[1]

Charles Finney was born in 1792 into an old New England family. He grew up in New York state, and as a young man decided to study law. Neither of his parents "professed religion," nor was religion popular among his neighbors. In his memoirs he writes:

> I recollect very well that the ignorance of the preachers that I heard was such, that the people would return from meeting and spend a considerable time in irrepressible laughter at the strange mistakes which had been made and the absurdities which had been advanced.[2]

When he went to Adams, New York, to study law under the guidance of attorney Benjamin Wright, Finney stated that he was "almost as ignorant of religion as a heathen."[3] It was the ministry of

Presbyterian clergyman Rev. George Gale that first caused Finney to question and later to be concerned for his soul's eternal destiny. He began secretly to read the Bible, and on a Sunday evening in 1821 decided to settle the question once and for all. On the following Wednesday morning, as he approached the law office, an inward voice said to him, "What are you waiting for? Did you not promise to give your heart to God?" Finney's reply was, "Yes; I will accept it today, or I will die in the attempt."[4]

Because he was so shy and ashamed about praying out loud, Finney went out to the woods north of the village, thinking that being away from the eyes and ears of people would enable him to pour his heart out in prayer to God. He entered the woods with the resolve, "I will give my heart to God, or I will never come down from there."[5] But Finney fell into a deep despair when he found that no matter how he tried, even there he was unable to pray. His heart felt dead to God, and he concluded that God had given up on him.

As Finney lingered a Bible verse came to his mind: "And you will seek Me and find Me, when you search for Me with all your heart" (Jer. 29:13). He determined to believe and cried out, "Lord, I take You at Your Word!" Many other scriptures came to his mind regarding Jesus Christ and what He had done on the cross.

> I took them one after the other as infallible truth.... They did not seem so much to fall into my intellect as into my heart...and I seized hold of them, appropriated them, and fastened upon them with the grasp of a drowning man.[6]

Finney prayed this way for some time, and before he was aware of it he was on his feet walking back to town. He had wonderful peace of mind but even then said, "If I am ever converted, I will preach the Gospel."

Arriving in town, he had a new concern, thinking to himself, *What is this? I have not a particle of concern about my soul; and it must be that the Spirit has left me. I must have grieved the Holy Ghost entirely away for I never in my life was so far from being concerned about my own salvation.*[7] Finney tried unsuccessfully to recall his conviction and regain the feeling of laboring under the load of sin. But all consciousness of guilt had departed from him. He was perplexed over the spiritual tranquility that had taken possession of him and concluded that in his excitement he had grieved the Holy Spirit and committed the unpardonable sin.

That evening he had no appetite, so he went back to the office, took out his bass violin, and began to play and sing some sacred music. Finney described what happened next:

As soon as I began to sing those sacred words, I began to weep. It seems as if my heart was all liquid; and my feelings were in such a state that I could not hear my own voice in singing without causing my sensibilities to overflow. I wondered at this, and tried to suppress my tears, but could not. After trying in vain to suppress my tears, I put up my instrument and stopped singing.[8]

After dinner Finney and Benjamin Wright were moving furniture and books. When the moving was done, Wright left Finney alone.

I accompanied him to the door; and as I closed the door and turned around, my heart seemed to be liquid within me. All my feelings seemed to rise and flow out; and the utterance of my heart was, "I want to pour my soul out to God." The rising of my soul was so great that I rushed into the room [in the] back of the front office, to pray.

There was no fire, and no light, in the room; nevertheless it appeared to me as if it were perfectly light. As I went in and shut the door after me, it seemed as if I met the Lord Jesus Christ face to face. It did not occur to me then, nor did it for some time afterward, that it was wholly a mental state. On the contrary it seemed to me that I saw him as I would see any other man. He said nothing, but looked at me in such a manner as to break me right down at his feet. I have always since regarded this as a most remarkable state of mind; for it seemed to me a reality, that he stood before me, and I fell down at his feet and poured out my soul to him. I wept aloud like a child, and made such confessions as I could with my choked utterance. It seemed to me that I bathed his feet with my tears; and yet I had no distinct impression that I touched him, that I recollect.

Finney continued in that state for quite a while. He says in his auto-biography that his mind was too much absorbed with the encounter to recollect anything that was said. Eventually, his mind became calm enough to break off from the interview, and he returned to the front office. There he found that the fire he had made of large wood was nearly burned out. Assuming the encounter was over he intended to sit down and reflect on what he had experienced.

But as I turned and was about to take a seat by the fire, I received a mighty baptism of the Holy Ghost. Without any expectation of it, without ever having the thought in my mind that there was any such thing for me, without any recollection that I had ever heard the thing mentioned by any person in the world, the Holy Spirit descended upon me in a manner that seemed to go through me, body and soul. I could feel the impression, like a wave of electricity, going through and through me. Indeed it seemed to come in waves and waves of liquid love for I could not express it in any other way. It seemed like the very breath of God. I can recollect distinctly that it seemed to fan me, like immense wings.

No words can express the wonderful love that was shed abroad in my heart. I wept aloud with joy and love; and I do not know but I should say, I literally bellowed out the unutterable gushings of my heart. These waves came over me, and over me, and over me, one after the other, until I recollect I cried out, "I shall die if these waves continue to pass over me." I said, "Lord, I cannot bear any more"; yet I had no fear of death. How long I continued in this state, with this baptism continuing to roll over me and go through me, I do not know.

It was late that evening when a member of the choir came into the office to visit Finney. He found the lawyer on the floor by the fireplace weeping loudly. "Mr. Finney," he called out, "what ails you?" The young lawyer could not answer him for some time. "Are you in pain?" the man continued to ask.

Finney gathered himself up as best he could and replied, "No, but so happy that I cannot live."

The astonished visitor hurriedly left the office to fetch one of the elders of the church from his office across the street. This elder had been carefully watching the skeptical lawyer. He was a serious man who had probably laughed before, but if he had no one could remember it. When this elder came in, Finney was still on the floor, very much in the same state in which the young choir member had found him. The stoic elder began to question Finney concerning his unseemly behavior. The effect on the church elder was astounding. In Finney's words:

> He [the elder] asked me how I felt, and I began to tell him. Instead of saying anything, he fell into a most spasmodic laughter. It seemed as if it was impossible for him to keep from laughing from the very bottom of his heart.[9]

Even after this incredible encounter, Finney still had reservations and questions. "Notwithstanding the baptism I had received...I went to bed without feeling sure that my peace was made with God." Finney tried to go to sleep that night but would wake up again and again with his heart overflowing with love:

> When I awoke in the morning the sun had risen, and was pouring a clear light into my room....Instantly, the baptism that I had received the night before, returned upon me in the same manner. I arose upon my knees in the bed and wept aloud with joy, and remained for some time too much overwhelmed with the baptism of the Spirit to do anything but pour out my soul to God. It seemed as if this morning's baptism was accompanied with a gentle reproof, and the Spirit seemed to say to me, "Will you doubt?" "Will you doubt?" I cried, "No! I will not doubt; I cannot doubt." He then cleared the subject up so much to my

mind that it was in fact impossible for me to doubt that the Spirit of God had taken possession of my soul.

In this state I was taught the doctrine of justification by faith, as a present experience. That doctrine had never taken any such possession of my mind, that I had ever viewed it distinctly as a fundamental doctrine of the Gospel. Indeed, I did not know at all what it meant in the proper sense. But I could now see and understand what was meant by the passage, "Being justified by faith, we have peace with God through our Lord Jesus Christ." I could see that the moment I believed, while up in the woods, all sense of condemnation had entirely dropped out of my mind; and that from that moment I could not feel a sense of guilt or condemnation by any effort that I could make. My sense of guilt was gone; my sins were gone; and I do not think I felt any more sense of guilt than if I never had sinned.[10]

This extraordinary encounter with God was the defining moment in Charles Finney's life. But it was also an event that affected the destinies of hundreds of thousands of people and that indirectly led to the most significant series of events in American history.

On the morning following the encounter Finney, as always, went to his office. When the law firm's senior partner arrived, Finney was still feeling waves of God's love and the assurance of eternal salvation. He could not help but speak a few words to his superior, whom he refers to as "Squire W-----," on the subject of his salvation. The squire looked at the young lawyer with astonishment and said not a word. Finney's words had pierced him like a sword and "he did not recover until he was converted."

Soon afterwards "Deacon B------" came into the office and said, "Mr. Finney, do you recollect that my cause is to be tried at ten o'clock this morning? I suppose you are ready?"

Finney replied, "Deacon B------, I have a retainer from the Lord Jesus Christ to plead his cause, and I cannot plead yours."

Before the morning was over, Finney had left the office to tell everyone he met about what had happened to him and about the gospel of Jesus Christ:

> I had the impression, which has never left my mind, that God wanted me to preach the Gospel, and that I must begin immediately.[11]

Like Peter who left his fishing nets to follow Jesus, and like Matthew the tax collector who left his money table, Finney became a preacher and never practiced law again. He became the greatest and most effective evangelist the American continent has ever known. It was largely due to Finney's preaching that 1831 is considered the greatest year of spiritual awakening in United States history.

Finney's social conscience, which was perpetuated by the school he founded, Oberlin College, had a major part in changing American culture. It set in motion the anti-slavery movement, which led to Lincoln's Emancipation Proclamation, the thirteenth amendment abolishing slavery, and the fifteenth amendment ensuring all races the right to vote. In 1841 Oberlin was the first college in America to grant a degree to a woman. Finney's ideas and his influence through Oberlin College were a catalyst for the women's rights movement, which eventually led to the nineteenth amendment guaranteeing equal rights to women.

EIGHTEEN

Harriet Tubman
ENGINEER ON THE UNDERGROUND RAILROAD
1849-1864

*T*he events surrounding the Civil War were the most tragic and ironic in all of American history. Often these kinds of settings serve as a stage on which the greatest examples of mankind's courage and corruption are played out. And so it was on both sides. Two of the most respected and renowned figures in American history are Abraham Lincoln and Robert E. Lee.

Perhaps one of the greatest of all American heroines was born a slave in 1820. Harriet Tubman has been likened by historians to Joan of Arc, to Florence Nightingale, and, more recently, to Raoul Wallenberg or Oskar Schindler.

After her escape to the North in 1849, Harriet Tubman began to make clandestine trips back into the South to lead small bands of runaway slaves on the treacherous, thousand-mile journey to freedom in Canada. Suddenly and mysteriously on a dark night she would appear at the door of a slave cabin where a trembling band anxiously awaited their deliverer. Among slaves she was known as "Moses." Hiding by day and traveling by night, scaling rugged mountains and fording rivers, she led the slaves through places that their pursuers wouldn't follow. The babies were drugged with paregoric to keep them from crying and giving away their hiding places. The trip was so hard that occasionally a man would complain that he could go no farther and desired to follow his steps back to the old home. Then Harriet's revolver would come out, and while pointing it at his head, she would say, "Dead niggers tell no tales; you go on or die!" In this way she "encouraged" them to drag their weary limbs on northward.[1]

Harriet's courageous efforts helped lay the tracks of what came to be known as the Underground Railroad, a network of people who helped slaves escape northward to Canada or who opened their homes as places of hiding, rest, and refreshment along the way. Though descriptions of Harriet and those she conducted northward were posted everywhere, Thomas Garrett, whose home was a stop on the Railroad, wrote, "No slave who placed himself under her care was ever arrested."[2]

Harriet made nineteen trips back to the slave states and by 1864 had escorted more than three hundred slaves to their freedom. Harriet herself, consequently, had become the South's most wanted criminal. The reward for her capture rose to $40,000, a sum equivalent to more than $700,000 in today's currency. Once when Harriet was traveling north in a railroad car, there was an "advertisement" (a "wanted" poster) posted right above her head with her description on it. Harriet couldn't read or write, but she could sense the suspicion of her fellow passengers. At the next station she quickly jumped off and caught a southbound train. Who would suspect anyone traveling south to be a runaway slave?

Harriet's life was full of acts of cunning, bravery, and determination. She did in real life what most of us only watch action heroes do in the movies. On one occasion she traveled south back to the town where she had only recently been a slave. She went to the marketplace with a sunbonnet pulled down over her face, walking bent over, pretending to be an old woman. At one point the man who had once hired her from her master passed by, unaware that he stood right next to the infamous runaway slave who had assisted so many in escaping to the North.

Harriet's astonishing boldness and craftiness were surpassed only by her faith and sense of divine guidance. Once, when she was advised that the risks of a journey to the South were too great, she said:

Now look yer! John saw de City, didn't he?... He saw twelve gates, didn't he? Three of dose gates was on de north; three of 'em was on de east; an' three of 'em was on de west; but dere was three more, an' dem was on de south; an' I reckon, if dey kill me down dere, I'll git into one of dem gates, don't you?[3]

Harriet fully expected God himself to meet her at every turn. She never knew a time when she did not possess that all-abiding confidence in God. As a slave she even spent time praying for the master who had treated her so cruelly. She told Sarah Bradford, her earliest biographer:

As I lay so sick on my bed, from Christmas till March, I was always praying for poor ole master. 'Pears like I didn't do nothing but pray for ole master. "Oh, Lord, convert ole master; Oh, dear Lord, change dat man's heart, and make him a Christian." And all the time he was bringing men to look at me, and dey stood there saying what dey would give, and what dey would take, and all I could say was, "Oh, Lord, convert ole master." Den I heard dat as soon as I was able to move I was to be sent with my brudders, in the chain-gang to de far South. Then I changed my prayer, and I said, "Lord, if you ain't never going to change dat man's heart, kill him, Lord, and take him out of de way, so he won't do no more mischief." Next ting I heard ole master was dead; and he died just as he lived, a wicked, bad man. Oh, den it 'peared like I would give de world full of silver and gold, if I had, to bring dat pore soul back. I would give myself; I would give eberyting! But he was gone, I couldn't pray for him no more.[4]

Harriet's was not a religion of formal morning and evening prayers. When she felt a need, she simply told God of it and trusted that the matter was settled. Again to Mrs. Bradford she said:

'Pears like, I prayed all de time about my work, eberywhere; I was always talking to de Lord. When I went to the horse-trough to wash my face, and took up de water in my hands, I said, "Oh, Lord, wash me, make me clean." When I took up de towel to wipe my face and hands, I cried, "Oh, Lord, for Jesus sake, wipe away all my sins!" When I took up de broom and began to sweep, I groaned, "Oh, Lord, clar and clean"; but I can't pray no more for pore ole master.[5]

None of the slaves were sure what would happen to them after the death of Harriet's master. The inward voice that was to help her evade her captors for the next fifteen years began whispering to her, "Arise, flee for your life!" In a vision she saw the horsemen coming, and heard the shrieks of women and children as they were being torn from each other and carried off to places no one knew. Harriet saw beckoning hands motioning her to come. She seemed to see a line dividing the land of slavery from the land of freedom, and on the other side of that line she saw people waiting to welcome her. Soon after, Harriet escaped alone, with only the North Star for her guide.

A Mr. Sanborn wrote of Harriet's activities in an account for *The Boston Commonwealth* in 1863 and mentioned one of her visions:

Between 1852 and 1857, she made but two of these journeys, in consequence partly of the increased vigilance of the slave-holders, who had suffered so much by the loss of their property. A great reward was offered for her capture and she several times was on the point of being taken, but always escaped by her quick wit, or by "warnings" from Heaven—for it is time to notice one singular trait in her character. She is the most shrewd and practical person in the world, yet she is a firm believer in dreams and warnings. She declares that before her escape from slavery, she used to dream of flying over fields and towns, and rivers and mountains, looking down upon them "like a bird," and reaching at last a great fence, or sometimes a river, over which she would try to fly, "but it 'peared like I wouldn't hab de strength, and jes as I was sinkin' down, dere would be ladies all drest in white ober dere, and dey would put out dere arms and pull me 'cross." There is nothing strange in this, perhaps, but she declares that when she came North she remembered these very places and those she had seen in her dreams, and many of the ladies who befriended her were those she had been helped by in her vision.[6]

On one of her journeys, Harriet was heading north with a company of slaves and they were being hotly pursued by a number of men. Suddenly she received one of her divine warnings. "Chillen," she said, "we must stop here and cross dis ribber." The river was wide and moving rapidly, and some of the escaping slaves couldn't swim. Nevertheless, Harriet was not one to hesitate, and they all followed her. Later, Harriet told Mrs. Bradford that she considered the crossing quite miraculous: "Missus, de water never came above my chin; when we thought surely we were all going under, it became shallower and shallower, and we came out safe on the odder side." They also found out later that a few hundred yards ahead, on the path they had originally planned to take, officers who had been forewarned of their coming were waiting for them.[7]

Before the Civil War, while staying with the Rev. Henry Garnet in New York, Harriet had another nighttime vision of the emancipation of her people. She rose singing, "My people are free! My people are free!" She came down to breakfast singing the words in a sort of ecstasy. The dream or vision had filled her whole soul, and she was unable to eat.

Rev. Garnet said to her, "Oh, Harriet! Harriet! You've come to torment us before the time; do cease this noise! My grandchildren may see the day of the emancipation of our people, but you and I will never see it."

"I tell you, sir, you'll see it, and you'll see it soon. My people are free! My people are free!"

When, three years later, President Lincoln emancipated the slaves by proclamation, there was a great jubilee among the friends of the slaves. Harriet was continually asked, "Why do you not join with the rest in their rejoicing?"

"Oh," she answered, "I had my jubilee three years ago. I rejoiced all I could den; I can't rejoice no more."[8]

All the many members of Harriet's family were rescued with the exception of one sister and her two children. In the process hundreds of others were saved as well.

There is a great irony in Harriet Tubman's story. Several years after her daring rescue missions, Harriet paid a lawyer five dollars to look up the will of her mother's first master. After searching through sixty-five years of records, he found the will in which a black slave girl named Ritty (Harriet's mother) was given by the master to his grand-daughter, Mary Patterson. However, Ms. Patterson died soon after, unmarried and with no heirs. Since there was no provision in the will for Ritty, legally she and all her descendants were, at that point, emancipated. But Ritty was never told of her right to go free, and she and her family remained slaves until Harriet, years later, escorted them one by one to safety. Harriet, whom her people called "Moses," was thus in one more way like Moses in the Bible: Had she not herself once lived in the land of bondage and seen the plight of her people, perhaps she would never have returned and become their great deliverer.[9]

Harriet Beecher Stowe

AUTHOR OF *UNCLE TOM'S CABIN*

FEBRUARY 2, 1851

Never has a single novel had such an effect on a nation and its course in history as did *Uncle Tom's Cabin* have on America. Many historians note that, more than any other single factor, the pen of Harriet Beecher Stowe brought on the Civil War and, with it, the emancipation of more than four million slaves. In 1862, at a private White House meeting, President Abraham Lincoln is reported to have greeted Harriet by saying, "Why, Mrs. Stowe, right glad to see you! So, you're the little woman who wrote the book that made this great war!"

Harriet grew up as a typical nineteenth-century girl whose place and influence were supposed to be limited to the home. She was born in an era when boys were what really mattered—because they were the ones who could possibly grow up to be ordained ministers. "Little Hattie" was lost in a family of renowned ministers. Her father, Lyman Beecher, was the most famous orator in America in a day when the clergy was the most respected of all occupations. Lyman's celebrity status as the greatest of preachers was passed on to Harriet's brother, Henry Ward Beecher. But with all their fame and influence, in time "Little Hattie's" prominence out-shone and out-lasted them all.

As one can imagine, Harriet heard a lot of preaching while growing up. She admitted privately, though, that her father's sermons were to her "as unintelligible as if he had spoken in Choctaw."[1] On occasion, however, Rev. Beecher would put away his notes and speak extemporaneously. It was on one such occasion, as he commented on the words from the Gospel of John, "Behold, I call you no longer servants, but friends," that he got the attention of his fourteen-year-old daughter. After the sermon Harriet crept into her father's study, fell to her knees beside him, and whispered, "Father, I have given myself to Jesus, and He has taken me."

With teary eyes her father gathered her up, saying, "Is it so? Then has a new flower blossomed in the kingdom this day."[2]

In the following years Harriet went through what theologians of her day called "the dark night of the soul." She questioned her faith, her calling, and her relationship with God. Though she dutifully went through the religious motions, for several years the self-doubt and introspection drained from her the joy she had received that summer Sunday in 1825.

Little by little Harriet found her way back to her relationship with God. She wrote to her brother, Edward:

All through the day...everything has a tendency to destroy the calmness of mind gained by communion with God. One flatters me, another is angry with me, another is unjust to me.... It matters little what service God has for me.... I do not mean to live in vain. He has given me talents, and I will lay them at His feet, well satisfied if He will accept them. All my powers He can enlarge. He made my mind, and He can teach me to cultivate and exert its faculties.[3]

In 1851 Calvin Stowe and his wife, Harriet Beecher Stowe, moved from Cincinnati to Brunswick, Maine, where Calvin had accepted a professorship at Bowdoin College. Things were developing in Washington that alarmed the Stowes and all of those in the North who opposed slavery. There had been a great power struggle between the slave states and the free states over newly formed territories. The California Compromise admitted California to the Union as a free state and, in return, the Fugitive Slave Act prevented slaves from becoming free just by crossing the border into free territory. There were harsh punishments for runaway slaves and for whites who aided them. Bounty hunters were allowed to capture runaways and return them to their "owners."

Soon after the Fugitive Slave Act became law, Harriet began to hear of its results in letter after letter from her sister-in-law, Isabella, who lived in Boston. The city government in Boston not only cooperated with the slave-catchers, it was in business with them! Former slaves were hiding out like the Christians in the catacombs of Rome. Because escaped slaves had married into Boston's free-black community, families were being torn apart. Blacks who were genuinely free were being kidnapped and "sold down the river" as runaway slaves.[4]

In Maine, Harriet continued with her daily duties of running a house and raising children, far removed from the things she heard were going on in Boston. In that remote area she could avoid having to face the slavery issue. Isabella wrote to Harriet, "Hattie, if I could use a pen as you can, I would write something that would make this whole nation feel what an accursed thing slavery is!" Harriet crumpled the letter in her hand as she said to herself, "God helping me, I will write something. I will if I live."[5]

In January 1851, Harriet's brother, Henry Ward Beecher, was on the lecture circuit. After giving an address in Boston, he got on a train to visit his sister in Maine. The main mission of Henry's ministry was to expose the evils of slavery. Harriet and Henry sat up and talked all night. Henry's passion had ignited Harriet. When he left, though, Harriet was again consumed with her children and her household duties. Even though she felt far removed from the real battle of ideas taking place in Boston, Washington, and New York, Harriet never lost the desire to be used by God to show the nation the horrors of the institution of slavery.

On the following Sunday morning Harriet sat in the cold College Church at Brunswick with her children. It was Communion Sunday, a service that Harriet always loved. But on this particular Sunday Harriet was barely paying attention as the ritual went on. She drifted off into a kind of trance. Suddenly, like the unrolling of a picture, a scene passed before her eyes. An old slave was being beaten to death by two of his own race. A white man, the overseer, lounged nearby, his face twisted with hate as he urged the killers on. Harriet wondered what it was the slave had done. The old black man never made a sound, but his face was noble and full of pity even for those who beat him. Finally, he collapsed to the ground and died.[6]

The vision left Harriet weak and shaken, and she could hardly keep from weeping aloud. She walked home with her children, skipped the Sunday dinner, and began to write down the vision that had been blown into her mind as by the rushing of a mighty wind. The words were pouring out of her head, through the pen, and onto the paper. When all of her paper ran out, Harriet found some left-over brown grocery wrapping paper and continued to write.

After some time, Harriet put down her pen and went to see to the children's dinner. After the meal she herded them into the sitting room and read aloud what she had written. Her son, Charles Edward Stowe, wrote in his biography of his mother, "Her two little ones of ten and twelve years of age broke into convulsions of weeping, one of them saying through his sobs, "Oh, mamma! Slavery is the most cruel thing in the world."[7]

Harriet reread the hurriedly written script the next day and was shocked that it had come from her own hand. It was nothing like anything she had wanted to write. But she couldn't get the vision out of her mind, so she began writing *Uncle Tom's Cabin* as a short story. She originally thought it would take only a couple of weeks. But the story had taken over Harriet, and after a couple of months, she realized it was becoming a novel. Portions of the story were published in a monthly periodical, *The National Era*.

In January 1852, a year after Harriet's vision, John P. Jewett of Boston had the forty-five chapter manuscript ready for publication. But Jewett wasn't sure it would sell and suggested that the Stowes back the cost of production in exchange for 50 percent of the profits. They finally settled on a 10 percent royalty and Jewett, with reservations, sent the book to the presses.

Three thousand copies of *Uncle Tom's Cabin* were sold on the first day. The entire first printing sold out by the end of the second day. Even before the first reviews were published, the third and fourth printings were sold out. Jewett could not keep up with the orders even though he ran the printing presses day and night, six days a week. Many tributes were written to the author, including one by Quaker poet John Greenlead Whittier. Henry Wadsworth Longfellow considered the book a great triumph. It found its way into almost every household in both America and England. During a trip to England, Harriet found herself in an unofficial meeting with Queen Victoria. *Uncle Tom's Cabin* was, of course, banned in the South. Samuel Green, a free black of Dorchester County, Maryland, was sentenced to ten years in the Maryland State Prison for possessing a copy of the book.[8]

The power of Harriet Beecher Stowe's pen had started a great moral and civil revolution. Because of the original vision and the consistent inspiration throughout the year of 1851, Harriet was always quick to say that it was God who wrote *Uncle Tom's Cabin;* she had only set down the words.

TWENTY

Abraham Lincoln
SIXTEENTH PRESIDENT OF THE UNITED STATES
APRIL 1865

*A*braham Lincoln is one of the most interesting, revered, and influential individuals in history. Carl Sandburg, who authored a six-volume biography of Lincoln, said, "A current of mysticism in Lincoln seemed to run parallel with a strain of rationalism." He was a lawyer, a debater, but also a man who believed it was the providence of the Almighty driving him and the events with which he found himself caught up.

In 1837, when Lincoln was twenty-eight years old, he went with some friends to a camp meeting revival of the Methodist Episcopal Church. As they were discussing the sermon on the way home, Lincoln said:

> It was the most instructive sermon I have ever heard. I firmly believe his interpretation of prophecy, especially about the breaking down of civil and religious tyrannies; and, odd as it may seem, I was deeply impressed that I should be somehow strangely mixed up with them.[1]

The Civil War era is considered by many to be the most emotionally charged period of American history. And yet Lincoln believed the entire bloody conflict was God's will. In the second year of the war, 1862, Lincoln wrote a note to himself. John Hay, assistant secretary to Lincoln, copied down the personal memorandum:

In the present civil war it is quite possible that God's purpose is something different from the purpose of either party; and yet the human instrumentalities, working just as they do, are of the best adaptation to effect his purpose. I am almost ready to say that this is probably true; that God wills this contest, and wills that it shall not yet end.[2]

By 1864, two years later, Lincoln's ideas about sovereignty and national atonement had become his convictions. His second inaugural address is etched in stone on the wall of the Lincoln Memorial in Washington. In that address he said that the Civil War was a judgment from God for the offense of slavery: "He gives to both North and South this terrible war, as the woe due to those by whom the offense came." He suggested that perhaps the war continued because there was some act of national atonement taking place:

Fondly do we hope—fervently do we pray—that this mighty scourge of war may speedily pass away. Yet, if God wills that it continue until all the wealth piled by the bondman's two hundred and fifty years of unrequited toil shall be sunk, and until every drop of blood drawn with the lash shall be paid by another drawn with the sword, as was said three thousand years ago, so still it must be said, "The judgments of the Lord are true and righteous altogether."[3]

In the Bible, particularly in the Old Testament, there are numerous stories of leaders being either promoted by God's grace or deposed by His judgment. Even though Lincoln had never supported slavery himself, as the chief representative of the United States he felt that he would personally suffer as a consequence of the national sin of slavery. Whether or not that is true, there remains no doubt Lincoln did have a sense of the divine purpose for his life and believed that death by assassination was his destiny. He felt that it was somehow to be a part of God's divine justice. On June 9, 1864, the Reverend Charles Chiniquy, who had known Lincoln in Illinois, paid his last visit to the president and spent considerable time with him talking about the threats of an assassination. Lincoln opened his Bible to Deuteronomy chapter 3 and read the story of Moses asking God to allow him to see the Promised Land (see Deuteronomy 3:23-27). He commented to Rev. Chiniquy:

> Has He not taken me from my poor log cabin, by the hand, as He did of Moses in the reeds of the Nile, to put me at the head of the greatest and most blessed of modern nations?...Has not God granted me a privilege, which was not granted to any living man, when I broke the fetters of 4,000,000 men, and made them free?
>
> Now I see the end of this terrible conflict, with the same joy of Moses...and I pray my God to grant me to see the days of peace and untold prosperity...as Moses asked God to see the other side of Jordan, and enter the Promised Land.
>
> Yes! Every time that my soul goes to God to ask the favor of

seeing the other side of Jordan…do you know that there is a still but solemn voice which tells me that I will see those things only from a long distance, and that I will be among the dead when the nation…will cross the Jordan; and why so?

Why did God Almighty refuse to Moses the favor of crossing the Jordan, and entering the Promised Land? It was on account of the nation's sins! That law of Divine retribution and justice, by which one must suffer for another, is surely a terrible mystery. But it is a fact which no man who has any intelligence can deny. Moses, who knew that law, though he probably did not understand it better than we do, calmly says to the people: "God was wroth [angry] with me for your sakes" [Deuteronomy 3:26].

My fear is that the justice of God is not yet paid. When I look upon the rivers of tears and blood drawn by the lashes of the merciless masters from the veins of the very heart of those millions of defenseless slaves, these two hundred years…I fear that we are still far from the complete expiation.

It seems to me that the Lord wants today, as He wanted in the days of Moses, another victim—a victim which He has Himself chosen, anointed, and prepared for the sacrifice, by raising it above the rest of His people. I cannot conceal from you that my impression is that I am the victim….Just as the Lord heard no murmur from the lips of Moses, when He told him that he had to die before crossing the Jordan, for the sins of his people, so I hope and pray that He will hear no murmur from me when I fall for my nation's sake.

"Never had I heard such sublime words," said Chiniquy. "Every sentence had come to me as a hymn from heaven, reverberated by the echoes of the mountains of Pisgah and Calvary. I was beside myself. Bathed in tears, I tried to say something, but I could not utter a word."[4]

Lincoln was also a dreamer. He told of one recurring dream, of a vessel moving with great speed over the water toward an indefinite shore. That dream came to him on the eve of nearly every great and important event of the Civil War.

Lincoln's most notable dream came in April 1865. He kept it to himself for a few days. However, one evening Mary Todd Lincoln, Ward Hill Lamon, and two others were at the White House, and the subject of dreams came up. It led the President to share his haunting encounter of the previous week. That very evening Lamon wrote down as exactly as he could remember what Lincoln had said:

It seems strange how much there is in the Bible about dreams. There are, I think, some sixteen chapters in the Old Testament and four or five in the New in which dreams are mentioned; and there are many other passages scattered throughout the book which refer to visions. If we believe the Bible, we must accept the fact that in the old days God and His angels came to men in their sleep and made themselves known in dreams. Nowadays dreams are regarded as foolish, and are seldom told, except by old women and by young men and maidens in love.

Mrs. Lincoln at that point remarked, "Why, you look so dreadfully solemn; do you believe in dreams?"

Lincoln continued:

I can't say that I do, but I had one the other night which has haunted me ever since. After it occurred, the first time I opened the Bible, strange as it may appear, it was at the twenty-eighth chapter of Genesis, which relates the wonderful dream Jacob had. I turned to other passages, and seemed to encounter a dream or a vision wherever I looked. I kept on turning the leaves of the old book, and everywhere my eye fell upon passages recording matters strangely in keeping with my own thoughts—supernatural visit-ations, dreams, visions.

The President looked so serious and disturbed that Mrs. Lincoln exclaimed: "You frighten me! What is the matter?"

"I am afraid," said Mr. Lincoln, seeing the effect his words had upon his wife, "that I have done wrong to mention the subject at all; but somehow the thing has got possession of me, and, like Banquo's ghost, it will not down."

This set on fire Mrs. Lincoln's curiosity. Though saying she didn't believe in dreams, she kept at him to tell what it was he had seen in his sleep that now had such a hold on him. He hesitated, waited a little, then slowly began.

About ten days ago I retired very late. I had been up waiting for important dispatches from the front. I could not have been long in bed when I fell into a slumber, for I was very weary. I soon began to dream. There seemed to be a death-like stillness about me. Then I heard subdued sobs, as if a number of people were weeping. I thought I left my bed and wandered downstairs. Then the silence was broken by the same pitiful sobbing, but the mourners were invisible. I went from room to room; no living person was in sight, but the same mournful sounds of distress met me as I passed along. It was light in all the rooms; every object was familiar to me; but who were all the people who were grieving as if their hearts would break? I was puzzled and alarmed. What could be the meaning of all this? Determined to find the cause of a state of things so mysterious and so shocking, I kept on until I arrived at the East Room, which I entered. There I met with a sickening surprise. Before me was a catafalque, on which rested a corpse wrapped in funeral vestments. Around it were stationed soldiers who were acting as guards, and there was a throng of people, some gazing mournfully upon the corpse, whose face was covered, others weeping pitifully. "Who is dead in the White House?" I demanded of one of the soldiers. "The President," was his answer; "he was killed by an assassin!" Then came a loud burst of grief from the crowd, which awoke me from my dream. I slept no more that night; and although it was only a dream, I have been strangely annoyed by it ever since.

"That is horrid!" said Mrs. Lincoln. "I wish you had not told it. I am glad I don't believe in dreams, or I should be in terror from this time forth."

"Well," responded Mr. Lincoln thoughtfully, "It is only a dream, Mary. Let us say no more about it, and try to forget it."[5]

On April 9, 1865, Robert E. Lee surrendered to Grant at Appomattox, Virginia. In less than a week Lincoln would be dead. According to Mary Todd Lincoln, the last day he lived, April 14, was the happiest of his life. His very last moments were spent with her talking about his future plans. He said he wanted to visit the Holy Land and see those places hallowed by the footprints of the Savior. He was saying there was no city he so much desired to see as Jerusalem; and with those words half spoken on his tongue, Abraham Lincoln was shot.[6]

TWENTY-ONE

George Washington Carver
PROFESSOR OF THE PEANUT
1915

George Washington Carver was born the son of a slave woman who was owned by a Missouri farmer, Moses Carver. During the Civil War it was difficult for farmers to keep slaves in border states such as Missouri. Consequently, Moses Carver sent all his slaves, including George and his mother, to Arkansas.

After the war all of Carver's slaves disappeared except for George, who had been frail and sickly. The motherless child was returned to his former master's home and nursed back to health. George remained with the Carvers until he was about twelve, when he left to get an education.

George Washington Carver worked at odd jobs, supporting himself until he graduated from high school in Minneapolis, Kansas. He received a scholarship to Highland University, a small Kansas college. As instructed, Carver reported to the president's office by September 13, only to be informed that there had been a mistake: Highland did not accept black students.

Carver finally got into Simpson College in Indianola, Iowa, then transferred to Iowa State Agricultural College. After receiving his master's degree in 1896, Carver joined the faculty of Booker T. Washington's Tuskegee Institute in Tuskegee, Alabama. There Carver

111

devoted himself to research projects aimed at helping Southern agriculture. His goal was to prepare rural blacks to take advantage of their full citizenship by teaching them how to become skilled farmers.

During his early years Carver spent a lot of time working with farmers to improve their economic situation. He wrote articles and gave numerous speeches about the need to rotate crops in order to keep from depleting the soil of all its nutrients. A few listened, but many were reluctant.

The main cash crop in the South was cotton. But in 1902 the boll weevil migrated into Texas, devastating the cotton crop. Carver continually warned farmers in Alabama that the boll weevils were on their way and that they needed to be ready. If they planted peanuts and sweet potatoes, the spread of the boll weevil would be stopped, and in addition, those crops would replenish the soil's nutrients. But nobody wanted to even think about growing anything but cotton.

Just as Carver warned, the boll weevil chewed its way across Texas, Louisiana, and Mississippi, and finally arrived in Alabama. And just as Carver predicted, in 1914 the Alabama crops were completely destroyed—except, that is, the peanut and sweet potato crops at Tuskegee Institute.

Letters began to pour in to Carver at Tuskegee. People were now ready to listen, and at Carver's suggestion farmers began to plant peanuts. Carver's plan, however, began to backfire. There were so many peanuts being produced that nobody in the South or the North wanted to buy them. The price of peanuts fell to almost nothing.

"You're the biggest fool of all, Mister Carver," a man named Ambrose Harper said. And he reflected the sentiments of all the farmers who had followed Professor Carver's advice.

Carver retreated to his lab, where he could avoid the faces of students and friends.

"But somehow I knew I was not alone," said Carver. "Even in the silence and stillness, I felt another presence. Falling on my knees, I begged forgiveness and understanding from my Savior and Creator. And as I prayed, I was drawn to my feet. Out of the lab I went, into the nearby woodlands and fields."

"Oh, Mr. Creator," I asked softly, "why did You make this Universe?"

A wind stirred the trees a bit. "Your little mind asks too much," came the answer. "Ask something more your size."

"What was man made for?" I whispered.

Once more I seemed to hear a voice on the wind. "You are still asking too much, little man. Try once more."

I fell to my knees. "Dear Mr. Creator, why did You make the peanut?"

Once more the breezes rustled through the trees. "Now you are asking questions your own size. Together we will find the answers."

Quickly Carver sprang to his feet and ran back to the campus. He ordered two students to bring in all the peanuts they could carry. Behind locked doors he began to study the peanut.

"I knew my hands were guided by a force other than my own," said Carver. "God would show me practical ways to use His creation."[1]

Carver's research ultimately developed more than three hundred derivative products from peanuts, including cheese, milk, coffee, flour, ink, dyes, plastics, wood stains, soap, medicines, and cosmetics.

When Carver arrived at Tuskegee in 1896, the peanut was not even recognized as a crop. Within the next fifty years it became one of the six leading crops in the United States, and by 1940, the second largest cash crop in the South after cotton.

In 1931 Joseph Stalin invited Carver to oversee cotton production in southern Russia, but he declined. Thomas Edison tried to persuade Carver to come and work with him. Carver refused a $100,000 per year salary to continue his work at Tuskegee. He was visited by many powerful and famous people, including Franklin D. Roosevelt and Calvin Coolidge. He became friends with people such as Henry Ford and Mohandas Gandhi. He received many awards, but was always regarded with suspicion by the scientific community because he always insisted that God was his collaborator in the laboratory.[2]

Norman Vincent Peale
PASTOR, AUTHOR, AND PUBLISHER
SUMMER 1933

*I*n the 1960s there was an immensely popular television show called "This Is Your Life." Each guest to be honored was tricked by his or her friends into coming to the studio, where they would be taken by surprise to find themselves the guest of honor as their life was reviewed before a national television audience. The surprise element left them no chance to prepare for any questions the host, Ralph Edwards, might ask. But when Norman Vincent Peale made his unexpected appearance on "This Is Your Life" and Edwards asked him, "What was your greatest experience in life?" without hesitation Peale replied, "It happened on a bench in a garden in England."

Peale had been a young pastor at University Avenue Methodist Church in Syracuse, New York. He had served there for five years when in a short period of time he received two phone calls, both from pulpit committees inviting him to be their new pastor. One offer was from the First Methodist Church in Los Angeles, then one of the largest congregations in the denomination. The other call was from the Marble Collegiate Church at Fifth Avenue and 29th Street in New York City. The New York church had a distinguished history dating back to the early 1600s. In fact, it was the oldest continuously functioning Protestant church in the United States. The old church, however, had been in decline for some time. They hadn't had a pastor for three years, and the Sunday morning faithful had dwindled to about two hundred people sparsely scattered throughout the huge sanctuary. Peale described his dilemma:

> After some thirty days of indecision regarding these two churches, I came home for lunch one day and began going over the problem for possibly the hundredth time. My wife Ruth, a practical woman with strong and certain faith, declared that the time had come for an uninterrupted prayer session with the objective of reaching a decision. She insisted, therefore, that we both continue to pray until the answer came, and to do so then and there. I agreed and we must have prayed for two or three hours; indeed, we lost track of time.[1]

In the end, they both had their answer. Peale called the pulpit committee chairman at Marble Collegiate Church and confidently accepted the invitation.

The present church building was a beautiful old edifice that had been erected in 1854 when New York's Fifth Avenue was only a dirt road. It was in desperate need of all kinds of repairs. Not only were the needed repairs very expensive and the congregation small, but the country was in the depths of the Great Depression. Thousands were out of work, and many of the church members had lost everything.

What does a minister in such a situation say to a remnant of discouraged worshipers haunted by fear and hopelessness? The unavoidable sight of the nearly empty sanctuary was in itself depressing. There seemed to be two choices: to confirm their fears, that things were bad and were in fact going to get worse; or to begin to give people hope. Peale decided to try something new:

> To the handful who came to worship in the almost empty church, I began to stress a positive faith that God loved them and would help them no matter how tough things were. In Christ's name I assured people that by a positive and truly believing faith a new day would dawn, and that with the Lord's help each one could begin again.[2]

The congregation did indeed respond, but very slowly. Gradually, they began to come out of their gloomy thinking. The church began to grow, but the growth was slow and the going was difficult. Peale himself had become discouraged and fatigued by the stress of working in an impossible situation. The first summer after coming to Marble Collegiate Church, Peale and his wife took a much-needed vacation. They went to England and checked into the Station Hotel in the charming little town of Keswick.

The Peales tried to relax, Ruth more successfully than Norman. The man who would become known for his optimism wrote candidly about those days:

> I was disconsolate, low in spirit, plagued by self-doubt. We took long walks among the beautiful streams and hills of one of the world's loveliest areas....But to no avail for me. The gloom of New York and the desolate state of the church had pervasively seeped into my mind and discolored it. Despite my enthusiastic preaching back in New York, I was myself pretty low on optimism.[3]

The hotel was surrounded by magnificent English gardens. There was a particular bench at the far end of the gardens where the Peales would sit as Norman daily poured out his woes to his young wife. One day, sitting on that bench, Ruth decided that she had heard about enough. "Norman," she said, "you are my husband, but you are also my pastor. I sit in church and listen to you preach the gospel of Christ with love and enthusiasm. But to hear you talk now, I wonder if you actually have any faith at all."[4]

The sound rebuke was unpleasant; nevertheless, it had hit its mark in Norman.

"What you need to do," she continued, "is to surrender your church, your problems, your entire self to Christ. You have done this before, but do it again now, and perhaps even in greater depth.... And," she added forcefully, "you are going to sit right here on this bench until you make that surrender."[5]

Ruth Peale could be sweet, patient, and gentle, but Norman knew at this point that she meant business. He knew he had no choice but to start praying:

"Dear Lord Jesus," I prayed, "I cannot handle my life. I need help. I need You. I hereby with all my heart surrender my mind, my soul, my life to You. Use me as You will. Fill me with Your Holy Spirit."

We sat together, hand in hand. Then it happened; such peace as I would never have dreamed possible surged through me, and with it a burst of joy. It was like light, like glory. Suddenly every dark, gloomy shadow in my mind fled and a light like the most radiant morning took the place of those old, dark things, sweeping them out as with a huge broom.

I was elated. I leaped to my feet and began to pace up and down. "It's wonderful," I declared. "It's wonderful! Praise God! I love Jesus Christ, I love everybody, I love you," and I swept her into a fervent embrace. "Tell you what," I said, "let's go back home. Let's get to work. We're going to have the time of our life."

I can tell you in complete sincerity that from that moment life was never again the same.[6]

The Peales went back to New York with a new power and a revitalized faith. The church grew until the sanctuary and the balconies were filled on Sunday morning. Then they went to two services, which were soon both filled. Peale began a radio program called "The Art of Living." Later he wrote a manuscript that was rejected by several publishers. Years later it was resubmitted and published under a new title. *The Power of Positive Thinking* has been through dozens of printings and sold millions of copies. Norman and Ruth also founded *Guideposts* magazine, which today has a circulation of more than four million. Peale, reflecting on his success, said, "The only way in which I as a person was involved was that, through my complete surrender to Him at Keswick, I became more useful to Him as a channel."[7]

TWENTY THREE

Catherine Marshall

AUTHOR OF *CHRISTY*

SUMMER 1944

*C*atherine Marshall's life was momentous in many ways. Her mother, Leonora Haseltine Whitaker, was born in 1891 and grew up on a farm in North Carolina. At the age of eighteen Leonora volunteered for service as a schoolteacher with Dr. Edward Guerrant's mission in the Great Smoky Mountains. Her experiences with the mountain people in the area surrounding "The Cove" became the basis for Catherine Marshall's novel, *Christy. Christy* was later made into a televisions series for CBS, with actress Kellie Martin playing the title role.

For those who have seen the television series and have wondered—yes, Christy Huddleston (or Leonora Whitaker) did wind up marrying the young preacher. They eventually had three children: Bob, Emma, and Catherine.

Years later, just as her mother had, Catherine fell in love with a young minister. On the morning after their wedding, Rev. Peter Marshall was scheduled for an interview with the pulpit committee of the New York Avenue Presbyterian Church in Washington, D.C. It was two blocks from the White House, with historical ties that went back to the early days of the Republic. A year later the young minister finally accepted the invitation to be their pastor. Peter Marshall also became the chaplain of the U.S. Senate. The shy twenty-three-year-old girl, who had once fled up the back stairs to avoid involvement with people, now became the hostess for a steady stream of social functions attended by the most powerful people in the world. The life and untimely death of Rev. Peter Marshall are recounted in the book and movie entitled *A Man Called Peter.*

Catherine Marshall once wrote, "[The places] I met God had not been on the easy straightaways but on the turns when I least expected the revelation of His presence."[1] In 1943, three years after their son's birth, Catherine was stricken with tuberculosis. The doctor's prescription: total and complete rest. She was to move as little as possible. The two-year confinement to her bed was agonizing. How could a three-year-old understand why Mommy couldn't play? As time went on, Catherine even began to lose her sense of self-worth as a wife and a mother. But Peter Marshall once told Catherine that someday she would look back with gratitude on those bleak days as some of the richest of her life.

During this time Catherine learned a lot about faith, her relationship with God, and being honest with herself. She had also wrestled with what the Bible says about healing, and in the process, prayed sincerely to be healed. But after two years the doctor's report was that there was little progress. Finally Catherine prayed a prayer of surrender, "Lord, I understand no part of this, but if you want me to be an invalid for the rest of my life—well, it's up to You. I place myself in Your hands, for better or for worse. I ask only to serve You."[2] What happened after that is what Catherine Marshall said was "the most real and vivid experience" of her life.[3]

In the middle of that night I was awakened. The room was in total darkness. Instantly sensing something alive, electric in the room, I sat bolt upright in bed. Past all credible belief, suddenly, unaccountably, Christ was there, in Person, standing by the right side of my bed. I could see nothing but a deep, velvety blackness around me, but the bedroom was filled with an intensity of power, as if the Dynamo of the universe were there. Every nerve in my body tingled with it, as with a shock of electricity. I knew that Jesus was smiling at me tenderly, lovingly, whimsically—as though a trifle amused at my too—intense seriousness about myself. His attitude seemed to say, "Relax! There's not a thing wrong here that I can't take care of."

His personality held an amazing meld I had never before met in any one person: warm-hearted compassion and the light touch, yet unmistakable authority and kingliness. Instantly, my heart wanted to bow before Him in abject adoration.

Would He speak to me? I waited in awe for Him to say something momentous, to give me my marching orders.

"Go," He said in reply to my unspoken question, "Go, and tell your mother. That's easy enough, isn't it?"[4]

That was it. "Go tell your mother." Catherine wondered what her mother would think of being awakened in the middle of the night. But the encounter had made her aware of two things: the freedom of each person's will; and the importance of obedience. Catherine brushed aside the thoughts of her mother's reaction and swung her legs over the side of the bed. She stumbled though the darkness to the bedroom across the hall where her mother and father were sleeping. Catherine gently spoke to her mother, who immediately sat upright and nervously asked what was the matter.

"It's all right," Catherine reassured them. "I just want to tell you that I'll be all right now. It seemed important to tell you tonight."

When I returned to the bedroom, that vivid Presence was gone. I found myself more excited than I have ever been before or since and more wide awake. It was not until the first streaks of dawn appeared in the eastern sky that I slept again.[5]

The next day the extraordinary visitation was as vivid to Catherine as it had been during the night hours. When she returned to Washington for another scheduled x-ray, the doctors for the first time reported a notable improvement. Within six months the doctors pronounced Catherine completely well.

Catherine later commented on that night.

That night also gave me an understanding of Jesus' resurrected body and of the spiritual bodies we shall have after death. For in the bedroom at Seaview there was no vision as seen with the retinas of my eyes, no voice as heard with my human eardrums. No such crude equipment was needed to "see" Him, to "hear" every word He spoke, to catch every nuance of that compellingly vivid Personality. Just so shall it be in the next life.[6]

TWENTY-FOUR

Elizabeth (Betsie) ten Boom

RAVENSBRUCK PRISONER 66729
DECEMBER 1944

*I*n the late thirties and early forties, the armies of the German Third Reich rolled through Western Europe, crushing all opposition in their path. Hitler had instituted a plan calling for the extermination of all Jews in German occupied territories. Many people in Holland, like the ten Boom family, did all they could to help the Dutch Jews trying to hide from the Nazis. The ten Booms became part of an underground network, and their house became a safe haven for those on the run. A false wall was built in Corrie's bedroom on the top floor. Behind the wall was the hiding place.

Their clandestine hospitality was successful until they were eventually betrayed. The Gestapo raided the house, arresting the old watchmaker, Casper ten Boom, and his two daughters, Betsie and Corrie. The next morning they were loaded into a van and transported to Scheveningen prison. The six Jews hiding in the secret room were never captured. They remained in the cramped space for almost two weeks before escaping. Casper ten Boom died nine days after he was arrested.

The ten Boom sisters spent three months at Scheveningen, Betsie in a cell with other prisoners and Corrie in solitary confinement, before being sent to a concentration camp in Vught, Holland.

On June 6, 1944, the Allies landed at Normandy, and by September they had liberated a portion of Holland. As a result, countless numbers of Dutch prisoners were hastily loaded into boxcars and sent to concentration camps in Germany. Many of the women were sent to a camp north of Berlin called Ravensbruck, where they suffered unspeakable cruelty.

At Ravensbruck the first thing they did with new arrivals was to take all their possessions from them—even their names. From that point on, Corrie was prisoner 66730 and Betsie was 66729. Corrie saw that the women prisoners were being stripped and searched, then forced to walk naked into the showers before they were issued prison dress. Silently she prayed that God would spare their Bible, which she had in a small drawstring bag under her sweater.

As the ten Booms drew closer to the inspection line, Betsie pleaded to use the toilet. Impatiently the guard snapped at them to use the drain holes in the shower rooms, and the two women quickly got out of the inspection line and made their way to the showers.

"Quick! Take off your sweater!" Betsie urged her sister. She then took their most precious possession, the Bible, wrapped it in the sweater and put the bundle in a cockroach-infested corner.

The sisters returned and went through the showers with the rest of the women. They were afterwards issued the shabby prison garb and shoes. Corrie retrieved the bundle that contained her Bible, the book the Nazis called *Das Lugenbuch* (the book of lies). But there was no way the thin prison dress could hide the bundle. As each prisoner exited they were each thoroughly searched from head to toe by the S.S. guards. "Oh, Lord," Corrie prayed, "send your angels to surround us!"[1] Corrie later explained:

> The woman ahead of me was searched three times. Behind me, Betsie was searched. No hand touched me.
>
> At the exit door to the building was a second ordeal, a line of women guards examining each prisoner again. I slowed down as I reached them but the Aufseherin in charge shoved me roughly by the shoulder. "Move along! You're holding up the line!"[2]

And so the Bible went with Corrie and Betsie into Barracks 8, which was located next to the punishment barracks. From there, all day long and sometimes into the night came the noises of hell itself, the sounds of blows landing, screams, and people crying in agony. After two weeks the sisters were moved to a permanent barracks, which was so infest with fleas and which smelled so horrible from the backed-up toilets that the guards wouldn't even go inside. Consequently, Corrie and Betsie could read the Bible aloud without fear of the guards overhearing.

Eventually, Betsie became so weak and so sick that she could no longer stand. Her legs were paralyzed, so Corrie and a friend had to carry her to roll call. Finally, she was taken to the hospital. Shortly afterwards, she died.

Betsie had had a vision, or perhaps it was a dream from God, about the work they would carry on when they got out of Ravensbruck. She also told Corrie that the Lord had specifically said that they would both be home by New Year's Day. A week after Betsie's death, Corrie took her place at roll call, standing in the icy weather for the ordeal that began at 4:30 A.M each day.

A guard called out, "66730, come forward!"

Corrie and another prisoner named Tiny were instructed to stand alone in a designated spot by themselves for the entire three-hour roll call. In all likelihood, Corrie and Tiny had been sentenced to death. In that time Corrie shared with Tiny about the love of God and the gospel of Jesus Christ. Before dismissal Tiny had become a Christian.

Within a few days Corrie ten Boom was unexpectedly released through a clerical error; she returned to Holland.

One week later, all the women Corrie's age who were imprisoned at Ravensbruck were executed. Tiny became one of the 97,000 women who died in that camp.

It was New Year's Day, 1945. Betsie was right; her dream had come true: They had both gone home by the New Year.

TWENTY-FIVE

Martin Luther King, Jr.

CIVIL RIGHTS LEADER

JANUARY 27, 1956

*B*orn the son of a Baptist minister, M.L., as he was called, was an exceptional child in many ways. His strong positive self-image was reinforced by the praises and adulation that came from his parents and his maternal grandmother. Yet, M.L. was a painfully sensitive boy. Growing up in segregated Atlanta left many unforgettable impressions on him. He tried to commit suicide twice by jumping out of a second-story window. This occurred once when he thought his grandmother had been killed, and once when she actually died.

With a razor-sharp intellect, he breezed though school with little effort, periodically skipping grades, and entered Morehouse College at the age of fifteen. His plans were to become a lawyer or a doctor, but due to the influence of Benjamin Mays, president of Morehouse, Martin Luther King, Jr., chose the ministry. He graduated from Crozer Theological Seminary in 1951 and eventually received a Ph.D. in systematic theology from Boston College.

King's early resentment of white people softened as a result of his university experiences, but he never lost his disdain for segregation. At Crozer he was influenced by the writings of Walter Rauschenbusch, whose teachings emphasized that a socially relevant faith must deal with the whole man, body, soul, and spirit, and that Christians should work for the kingdom of God to come on earth as it is in heaven.[1]

After finishing his doctoral studies at Boston College, King became pastor of the Dexter Avenue Baptist Church in Montgomery, Alabama. He had no idea that in less than a year he would be the spokesman for a movement that would shake the nation.

On Thursday, December 1, 1955, a young black seamstress, Rosa Parks, boarded the Cleveland Avenue bus in downtown Montgomery. Not long after she took a seat in the front of the bus, she and three other black passengers were asked to move to the back to make room for white passengers who were boarding. They were sitting in the whites-only section. But by that time all the seats in the back of the bus had been taken. The other three black passengers moved, but Parks refused and was arrested for violating the Alabama segregation law.

Indeed, this was not the first such incident. Earlier that year a fifteen-year-old high school girl, Claudette Colvin, had been pulled off a bus, handcuffed, and taken to jail for refusing to give up her seat. Reverend King, who had arrived at the Dexter Avenue Church only a few months earlier, had been asked to serve on a committee that was to meet with the Montgomery City Lines bus company.[2]

A series of events were set in motion on the day of Rosa Parks' arrest that resulted in the most profound transformation of American culture since the Civil War. Word got around quickly about the arrest, and members of the Women's Political Council suggested that the time had come to boycott the buses. The word was spread in an unexpected way. Someone in the white community who was unsympathetic to the cause found a printed leaflet announcing the boycott and promptly gave it to the editor of the newspaper. The story about the planned boycott appeared on the front page of the Sunday paper—so everyone got the message.

The boycott of city buses lasted for an entire year. The young minister from the Dexter Avenue Baptist Church emerged as the spokesman for the boycott leadership. A month into the boycott, racial tensions that were high from the beginning began to turn violent. King, who also served as one of the many drivers in the elaborate volunteer transportation system, was arrested and sent to jail for allegedly driving 30 mph in a 25 mph zone. He was also by this time receiving a continuous stream of threats, including death threats. He began to feel the pressure, realizing that at any moment he could be killed.

Late one night in January 1956, after King had already gone to bed, the phone rang. An angry voice said, "Listen, nigger, we've taken all we want from you; before next week you'll be sorry you ever came to Montgomery." It's not easy to go back to sleep after a call like that. King later said:

> I hung up, but I couldn't go back to sleep. It seemed that all of my fears had come down on me at once. I had reached the saturation point.
>
> I got out of bed and began to walk the floor. Finally, I went to the kitchen and heated a pot of coffee. I was ready to give up. With my cup of coffee sitting untouched before me I tried to think of a way to move out of the picture without appearing a coward. In this state of exhaustion, when my courage had all but gone, I decided to take my problem to God. With my head in my hands, I bowed over the kitchen table and prayed aloud. The words I spoke to God

that midnight are still vivid in my memory. "I am here taking a stand for what I believe is right. But now I am afraid. The people are looking to me for leadership, and if I stand before them without strength and courage, they too will falter. I am at the end of my powers. I have nothing left. I've come to the point where I can't face it alone."

At that moment I experienced the presence of the Divine as I never experienced Him before. It seemed as though I could hear the quiet assurance of an inner voice saying, "Stand up for righteousness, stand up for truth; and God will be at your side forever." Almost at once my fears began to go. My uncertainty disappeared. I was ready to face anything.[3]

Reverend King had had enough, and was looking for a way out. But because of his extraordinary experience at the kitchen table, he stuck with his activist course, even though three nights later, on January 30, his house was dynamited. Fortunately his wife, Coretta, and his daughter were unhurt. In the years that followed, the movement led by King resulted in not only an agreement with the Montgomery City Lines but the Civil Rights Act of 1964 and the Voting Rights Act of 1965.

In 1964 Dr. King, at the age of thirty-five, was the youngest-ever recipient of the Nobel Peace Prize. On April 4, 1968, while in Memphis, Tennessee, assisting sanitation workers striking for the right to form a union, he was assassinated.

In the history of the United States, no one person has had a more profound influence on society and culture than Dr. Martin Luther King, Jr. How different would our world be had he given up back in 1956!

TWENTY-SIX

Norman Williams
PASSENGER ON PAN AM FLIGHT 206
MARCH 27, 1977

A terrorist bombing at the Las Palmas Airport on Grand Canary Island prompted the control tower to divert Pan American Flight 206 from New York to the Tenerife Island airport, sixty miles away. The small airport at Tenerife was overflowing with scores of unscheduled arrivals. What the full load of passengers on the Pan Am 747 were told would be a one-hour wait dragged on and on for more than four hours.

Meanwhile, a chain of events and decisions, some still unexplained, led to the worst airline disaster in history.

Norman Williams, president of the California College of Commerce, had shared lunch with his mother on the day of his departure from Los Angeles. Williams had a deep faith in God, as did his mother. When it came time to leave for the airport, Norman's mother said, "Let's pray." That wasn't unusual. "But this time," said Williams, "there was a quality I had never heard in her voice. I raised my head to look at her. Tears were streaming down her face."[1]

Dr. Williams, like most frequent travelers, had hoped that the seats next to him would be empty. But the Pan Am flight was completely packed. Many were older passengers from Leisure World, a retirement community in Orange County. Norman tried to get a seat near his business associate Ted Younes, but the seat behind was as close as he could get. It would prove to be a fateful separation.

After flying more than five thousand miles from Los Angeles to Tenerife, Flight 206 sat on the runway for four hours, waiting for clearance to complete the remaining sixty-mile flight to the Grand Canary Island. By this time there was a traffic jam of grounded 747s on the tarmac of the small airport.

Pan Am 206 finally received permission to taxi toward the runway, but it was blocked by the tail section of KLM Flight 4805, which was being refueled. It was nearly 5:00 P.M. and, to complicate an already difficult situation, a dense fog was rolling in. To make matters worse, the control tower at Tenerife had no ground radar, and had to rely on visual and radio communications.

After KLM 4805 completed its refueling, the control tower instructed its captain: "Taxi the full length of Runway 30, make a 180-degree turn and hold."

The tower then radioed Victor Grubbs, captain of Pan Am 206: "Follow KLM [4805] about three minutes behind and turn off at third intersection."

The taxiway that planes normally used to reach the end of the runway was clogged with parked 747s. So KLM 4805 was instructed to taxi straight up the eleven-thousand foot main runway, followed by Pan Am 206. The KLM was supposed to turn around at the end of the runway, then wait for the Pan Am plane to clear out of the way by turning onto a side access ramp.

Pan Am 206 moved up the runway at 6 mph, five hundred yards behind the first plane. But as the Pan Am 747 drew closer to the access ramps, the pilots became uncertain where to turn off. What appeared to be the third exit adjoined the runway at a 45-degree angle. However, it angled *away* from the direction Pan Am 206 was headed, which meant the jumbo jet would have to turn almost completely around before it could get off the runway.

Captain Grubbs quickly opted to turn off on the next ramp, which was readily accessible, and commented to his copilot: "This field is below takeoff minimum. When we get to the end of the runway, we are going to hold off until the weather improves."

Meanwhile, the KLM plane had reached the end of the runway, turned around, and was ready for takeoff. The captain radioed to the control tower: "Request air control clearance."

The reply came back from the tower: "To Papa Beacon, climb to 9,000, right turn to heading 040 until intercept 325 radial."

KLM signalled back: "We are now at takeoff."

Tower to KLM: "Stand by for takeoff clearance. I will call you back."

For some unexplained reason—whether they did not hear it or misunderstood it—the KLM flight crew never responded to this instruction. Pan Am 206, which was still on the runway, caught the signal.

Referring to the KLM plane, Captain Grubbs said to his copilot: "He's not cleared for takeoff."

At that moment, the control tower tried to verify Pan Am's location: "Clipper 1736, report clear of runway."

They signalled back: "Will report when clear of runway."

Tower to Pan Am: "Roger, thank you."

Tragically, the KLM pilot must have caught only the last half of the Pan Am signal: "...clear of runway."

Still moving down the runway through the misty fog, the Pan Am pilots could barely see the dim lights of the KLM. Suddenly Pan Am copilot Robert Bragg screamed, "He's moving!"

Pan Am Captain Grubbs to tower: "We're still on the runway!"

Copilot Bragg: "Get off! Get off!"

The giant KLM 747 was thundering at full power right at the Pan Am 747. Captain Grubbs jammed the throttles forward, trying to veer his plane off the runway. But the KLM was already rolling at 180 mph, and there was very little time. The KLM pilot pulled the control yoke all the way back in a desperate attempt to leap-frog the Pan Am, but his plane was sluggish with 142,000 pounds of jet fuel. In one horrifying moment, three hundred tons of aluminum, steel, and jet fuel slammed into Pan Am 206.

The nose of the KLM cleared the Pan Am, but the fuselage hit it right in the midsection. The KLM's number three engine took off the entire lounge section behind the Pan Am cockpit. The KLM hit the ground on the other side of the Pan Am, skidded around, and exploded.

None of the 249 passengers and crew on the KLM survived the crash.

Norman Williams, in seat 29C of the Pan Am, had felt the plane drop as its left wheels went off the runway pavement, followed a sec-

ond later by the impact. There was instant fire, with flames and fragments of white hot metal blasting through the cabin where Williams
sat. The ceiling fell. There was an explosion, screams, cursing, moan-
ing…and then silence. Williams described his feelings and the events
that followed that incredible moment:

> I felt like I had lived this moment before. The psychologists have
> a name for this phenomenon: *deja vu,* meaning "already seen."
> Maybe the hand of God had something to do with this strange
> familiarity. Was I closer to God at this moment and, therefore,
> closer to timelessness and an instant supply of calm, lucidity and
> superhuman strength?[2]
>
> I was on my feet. I don't remember unbuckling my seat belt.
> My first impulse was to help the old lady next to me. But she
> was not in her seat. Just gone. She and her daughter had col-
> lapsed downward as if into the floor, buried under debris.
>
> My next reaction was to turn to my partner, Ted. But Ted
> was not there, simply gone.[3]
>
> In that instant, I saw myself back at home holding the Bible
> with my mother. Don't ask me how, but I saw the tears in her eyes
> as she prayed for my safe return. At that moment I cried out, "In
> the name of Jesus, through Your shed blood, I stand upon Your
> Word." I began to move through the heaving exploding havoc. "I
> stand upon Your Word … stand upon Your Word … stand upon
> Your Word." I have had some marvelous spiritual experiences
> throughout my life, but I have never sensed the presence of the

Holy Spirit as I did in that indescribable fury.[4]

Then another explosion racked the plane. A lightning-like sheet of flame cremated human flesh and metal alike, vaporizing everything in its path.

Through the flames a huge object came hurtling directly at me. It was white hot. I threw up my arms in an automatic reflex. I felt unexplainably strong. It struck my arms and was deflected. I don't know what it was or how I could have stopped that huge object. Again I shouted, "I stand upon Your Word!" I turned and looked toward the back and saw what I shall never forget—bleeding faces, burning faces, stony faces. Within a few seconds everybody in the seats behind me with but one or two exceptions was already dead. I seemed separated from all of this, and I knew that my insulation from death was due to my prayers.

That hurtling metal had driven me back so I could see a light splotch through the smoke—a gash in the cabin ceiling and the sky visible through it. There was my escape hatch, but it was so high. How was my bone-tired, six-foot, 250-pound, overweight frame lifted approximately ten feet to grab the ragged edges of the blasted fuselage and hurl myself over the edge? How it happened, I may never know. But happen it did.[5]

From the top of the aircraft, Williams threw himself over the side onto the wing, which was covered with slippery jet fuel. He flung himself off the wing, dropped thirty feet to the ground, and hobbled away from the plane. Seconds later there was a massive explosion, and the entire Pan Am 747 was a fireball of twisted metal. Of the 394 people on board Pan Am Flight 206, 333 were killed, bringing the total death count to 592 people.

As Norman Williams limped away on a broken foot, praising God for sparing his life, a Bible verse came to mind: "When thou walkest through the fire, thou shalt not be burned; neither shall the flame kindle upon thee" (Isaiah 43:2, KJV).

TWENTY-SEVEN

"Pistol" Pete Maravich

BASKETBALL HALL OF FAMER
NOVEMBER 1982

*P*ete Maravich, wearing the same old pair of droopy socks every game, was one of the greatest and most exciting basketball players of all time. After twenty-five years he still holds the NCAA's highest season point average per game (44.5) and the highest career point average per game (44.2). He is the NCAA's all-time leading scorer with 3,667 points, even though he played fewer games than any of the NCAA's other top ten scorers, including the likes of Oscar Robertson, Elvin Hayes, and Larry Bird.

You would normally assume that such college basketball greatness would translate to success in the NBA, but that was not to be. Maravich's style of play didn't fit in on the professional level. The continual criticism from the media left him paranoid and shell-shocked. After ten years in the NBA his childlike imagination and zest for the game turned to cynical despair, which was manifest in ways such as radical views on food, medicine, and politics.[1]

In the years that followed his retirement from basketball, Maravich became increasingly depressed, bored, and anguished over his own life. For two years he remained in almost total seclusion, diving into one fad after another, looking for some kind of peace and fulfillment.

Finally, there came a divine encounter that rescued him from his sea of confusion and self-pity:

On a cool November evening in 1982, a chilling wind blew across Lake Pontchartrain as I sat watching television. I stared at the television screen, but my mind wandered far from the late movie. It was a time for introspection; a time for contemplating my past. Jaeson had long since been tucked into bed, and Jackie had turned in some time later.

For the most part this night was like every other night. I was living the good life, with every material thing I wanted; and I had a family who loved me. But the loneliness and guilt I felt was devastating.

Dad and Diana had been in touch by phone, concerned about my moodiness and silence; but not even a heart-to-heart talk with Dad had calmed the inner struggle.

I had quietly slipped into bed and tried to close my eyes. It was useless. The harder I tried to forget what was on my mind, the more graphic my imagination became. Dark and haunting images from the past surfaced. Try as I might, those images couldn't be dismissed.

The second hand moved slowly on the alarm clock. It was 2:00 A.M. My head pounded with activity, a myriad of thoughts racing through my mind. My conscience was bothering me as never before. At times I thought I might be dozing off, but a glance at the alarm clock showed that the hands had moved only a minute or two.

I recalled the night I had taken my first drink on the steps of the church, and how the first sip nearly ruined my life. I considered the effect it had on my mother and on our family in general. I remembered all the ugly things I'd done to people, and I recalled the friends and enemies I had made in college and in the pros. My thoughts wandered to all the rebellion I had toward God, my family, and others. All the horrible things I had said and the stupid things I had done seemed to be illuminated. No matter how hard I tried, I couldn't derail the thoughts.

Finally, I recognized that it was more than just thoughts running through my head. It was sin.

The night wore on, and as early morning approached, I knew I had to make things right with God. As I turned to find a comfortable position in the bed, I realized that the sheet was soaked with my sweat. Again, I glanced at the clock that now read 5:40 A.M. The guilt from the past was relentless and had become too heavy to handle alone, so I broke the silence with a prayer. The course my life had taken through the years had always clashed with the way God had intended, and it was time to admit it.

I cried out to God, saying, "I've cursed you and I've spit on you. I've mocked you and used your name in vain. I've kicked, punched, and laughed at you. Oh, God, can you forgive me, can you forgive me? Please, save me, please. I've had it with this life of mine. I've had it with all the world's answers for happiness. All of it, the money, fame, and things have left me so empty."

I remember the late sixties and the day in California when I rejected the idea of a personal relationship with Jesus Christ because of what it might do to interfere with my career goals. Now, sixteen years later, I wondered if God had forsaken me because of all the things I had done or not done. A deafening silence filled the dark room, and the tears I felt flowing down my cheeks were the tears of a spiritually broken man.

Suddenly, without warning, I heard a voice say, "Be strong. Lift thine own heart." The voice seemed to reverberate throughout the room. I looked up in shock and checked to see if Jackie and I were still alone. The only sound I heard was the loud thumping of my racing heart. What I'd heard hadn't come from within me. It was an audible voice!

I immediately awoke Jackie, startling her in the process. She was afraid someone was breaking into the house. "Did you hear what God said to me? You had to hear it!" I told her. "He said, 'Be strong. Lift thine own heart.'"

To my surprise, she reacted as if nothing out of the ordinary had happened. She closed her eyes and lay back on her pillow. "I didn't hear a thing, Pete," she answered in a sleepy voice muffled by the pillow.

Jackie had been through so many roller-coaster experiences with me and my searching. To her, my exclamation was nothing more than another wacky result of looking for my purpose in life. She figured it, too, would pass. She was really more interested in catching up on the sleep she was missing.

But this experience was so different from the rest! As I sat there in my excitement, I again recalled that day in California when I had rejected Christ. I recalled how my friend had received Christ into his life.

I prayed a simple prayer as best I could. "Jesus Christ, come into my life...forgive me of my sins. I believe with all my heart that you died for me and rose from the grave so I would have eternal life. Make me the person you want me to be."

Through this simple act of surrender, the void that once loomed so large was filled. From that moment on, my life was never to be the same.[2]

Pete Maravich was a completely different person after that evening. He was energized with a new sense of his relationship with God and with a sense of purpose. He became the father and husband he always wanted to be. He also dedicated himself to working with kids, trying to influence their lives and point them in the right direction. As a result of his influence, Press Maravich, Pete's father and college coach, also dedicated his life to Jesus Christ.

Though Maravich never gained the one thing for which he had spent most of his life striving, a championship ring, he did find peace and personal happiness. On May 5, 1987, five years after he retired from professional basketball, Pete Maravich was inducted into the Basketball Hall of Fame. On January 12, 1988, "Pistol Pete," at the age of forty, collapsed on a basketball court and died instantly of a heart attack.

TWENTY-EIGHT

Vladimir Slolvev, Oleg Atkov, and Leonod Kiaim

SOVIET COSMONAUTS
1984

Six Soviet cosmonauts said they witnessed the most awe-inspiring spectacle ever encountered in space: a band of glowing angels with wings as big as jumbo jets. Cosmonauts Vladimir Slolvev, Oleg Atkov, and Leonod Kiaim said that they first saw the celestial beings during their 155th day aboard Salyat 7 Space Station.

What we saw were seven giant figures in the shape of humans, but with wings and mist-like halos in the classic depiction of angels. Their faces were round with cherubic smiles.

Twelve days later the figures returned and were seen by three other Soviet scientists, including cosmonaut Svetlana Asvitskaya. "They were smiling," she said, "as though they shared a glorious secret."[1]

TWENTY-NINE

Dennis Byrd
DEFENSIVE END, NEW YORK JETS
DECEMBER 1992

*O*n a cold November afternoon in 1992, the New York Jets were playing the Kansas City Chiefs at Giants Stadium. Dennis Byrd was rushing the Chiefs' quarterback, David Kreig, from his defensive end position. Kreig saw the six-foot-five, 270-pound lineman coming at full speed and stepped forward. Byrd went right by the quarterback and collided with Scott Mersereau, another Jet lineman, rushing from the other defensive end position.

At that moment everything stopped for Dennis Byrd as he fell limply to the ground with a broken neck. He had suffered a "non-displacement, explosion fracture" of the fifth cervical vertebra. The extraordinary force literally exploded the vertebra, breaking it in four places and driving fragments of the bursting bone against the spinal cord. Because of the location and severity of the fracture, there was a good possibility that Dennis Byrd would be a quadriplegic for the rest of his life.

Dennis grew up in Oklahoma as the son of an ordained minister. He had become one of the Jets' most popular players. He was an outgoing, happy-go-lucky prankster, while at the same time a committed Christian.

On the way to the hospital Dennis and his wife, Angela, prayed together. He determined that no matter what happened he was going to be a witness for Jesus Christ in the uncertain days, years, or even lifetime of difficulties that lay ahead:

> There were trials ahead of me that I could not imagine, so many moments where my faith and strength would be tested, but none would be more crucial than the prayer we shared inside that ambulance. Because it was then and there that I found the inner core of peace that would see me through everything to come. It was at that moment en route to the hospital, that I turned everything over to the Lord, that I put it all in His hands.[1]

As soon as Dennis arrived at Manhattan's Lenox Hills Hospital, the doctors began to run all kinds of tests. They hooked up monitors, a catheter, and an IV. On Monday morning Dennis Byrd, who twenty-four hours earlier had been a perfect physical specimen, was a quadriplegic. The only parts of his body below the shoulders that he could control were his biceps. Other than that, he was limp.

Concerning that time Byrd said, "Jesus Christ had been with me during the past ten days more than He had ever been with me in my entire life. I knew I would need Him even more in the days ahead."

In the days that followed Byrd had to go through grueling therapy, bed sores, and a multitude of humiliating rituals. One of the most difficult things was not knowing how much movement he would regain...if any at all. Only one year before, a similar accident had left Mike Utley, defensive lineman for the Detroit Lions, a quadriplegic.

Almost a month after the injury something happened that, more than any of the occasional twitches in his body, gave Byrd hope and confidence for the future:

One afternoon, just before Christmas, Angela and Chris [Angela's brother] were in my room. We had all been reading the Bible together and praying, and now I was lying back resting while they sat nearby, talking to each other. I had my eyes closed. I was dog-tired, as usual, after another session downstairs, and I started sinking down into the gravity of all this. Usually I could keep myself on top of things. My willpower and faith and positive thinking kept me balanced, as if I was perched on top of a big ball. Occasionally, though, one of those things would begin to slip, I'd begin losing my balance, and the ball would start to roll over on me.

That's how I felt lying in bed that afternoon. I'd made a lot of progress, but I was still so far from doing anything close to walking. I couldn't even lift my leg. I could flex some muscles, but I couldn't make it move. And my hands were so limp. I wondered if I was truly strong enough to handle this. I wondered if I could take it.

And then a voice came to me, a voice as clear as any I'd ever heard. And it said, "Be strong, my son. You will walk again."

I was shocked. I started crying. Angela and Chris looked over and had no idea what was happening. Ange came over and held me, and asked me what was wrong, and I told her. Then they began crying, too. No moment in my life, before or since, was as strong as that one, the three of us crying together from the bottom of our souls, weeping with joy and awe, knowing that the Lord was with me, that He was with all of us.[2]

Dennis began to show faint signs that he might recover, nerve responses in his feet that were almost indetectable. He began the long and arduous process of rehabilitation and on September 7, 1993, opening day for the New York Jets in Giants Stadium, Dennis Byrd was able to walk out onto the field with all his former teammates.

In the next few years Dennis received many awards for his courageous comeback, including Father of the Year, the Jim Thorpe Award, and an honorary doctorate from Fairleigh Dickinson University. He is now working to establish the Dennis Byrd Foundation for the disabled.

Captain Scott O'Grady

31st Fighter Wing, USAF
Bosnia, June 6, 1995

*I*n June of 1995, F-16 pilot Captain Scott O'Grady, along with thirty-four other pilots from the 555th Squadron of the United States Air Force's 31st Fighter Wing, was stationed at Aviano Air Base in northeastern Italy. Their mission was to enforce the NATO no-fly zone in the skies over Bosnia.

"BASHER 52," Captain O'Grady's call name, had already racked up forty-six "Deny Flight" sorties over Bosnia, four of them with his new wingman, Bob ("Wilbur") Wright. The objective for the June 2 mission was to back up U.N. peacekeepers on the ground and to prevent anyone—Serbs, Croats, or Muslims—from using the air to project military power against the other warring factions. After more than a year of "Deny Flights" over Bosnia, hostile ground fire had taken down only one British Harrier. That pilot was returned on the same day by local Muslims. But things were now heating up. Three hundred fifty U.N. peacekeepers were being held hostage, and NATO had launched air strikes against Bosnian Serb munitions depots.

O'Grady and Wright were continuing their patrol after their first mid-air refueling, carefully avoiding the surface-to-air (SAM) threat-rings. They had no way of knowing that the Bosnian Serbs had secretly tractored an SA-6 SAM battery right into the path of their patrol.

At exactly 3:03 P.M. O'Grady's alarm went off indicating that he was being tracked by acquisition radar. Six seconds later a louder alarm went off, signaling that he had been locked onto by target-tracking radar, the type of radar that guides a missile, and which was probably already on its way. The words "COUNTER, COUNTER" squawked in his headset. O'Grady began to negotiate maneuvers that would push the F-16 to its limits. Three seconds later an SA-6 missile exploded between the two planes. O'Grady's plane was cut in two by a direct belly hit.

Having just refueled, his F-16 was like a flying gas tank. Surrounded by fire, Captain O'Grady prayed, "Dear God, please don't let me die now—don't let me die from this." With adrenaline pumping hard, O'Grady found the lever located between his legs and ejected himself from the plane, traveling 350 mph at twenty-six thousand feet.

As he floated down from twenty-four thousand feet, where he had manually opened the parachute, O'Grady could see soldiers in trucks arriving to capture their prize. He had no idea, if captured, whether he would be tortured, killed, or held hostage.

O'Grady came down only a short distance from troops searching for him. Releasing the parachute harness, he began moving as fast as he could away from them.

For the next five days Captain O'Grady evaded detection as he tried unsuccessfully to make radio contact with friendly forces. On the first day two men walked up to the very edge of his hiding spot. They almost stepped on him. "I don't know why they missed me," O'Grady commented later, "can't explain it, except that God veiled me from them."[1]

O'Grady prayed continually. "In Bosnia I caught a glimpse of God's love, and it was the most incredible experience of my life. I'd tapped into the brightest, most joyous feeling; I felt warmed by an everlasting flame. For all my physical complaints, I'd been on a spiritual high since that missile and I intersected."[2]

On two occasions during the days he was evading the Bosnian Serbs, O'Grady had something of a divine encounter:

The enemy chopper left my vicinity after fifteen minutes.... And then I shut my eyes, and something happened to make me realize that I wasn't outnumbered, after all—that I had more allies than I could count. I prayed, and I wasn't a solo. I had joined a huge chorus; I could hear prayers for me from throughout the world, from my family to the most remote, faceless stranger. There were no barriers of language, or politics, or even religion. There was only a rising tide of unity, and caring, and belief.[3]

On his third day of hiding O'Grady was praying again:

Before long I felt a definite presence. It grew more and more vivid, until I could see it, shimmering in my mind's eye. It's hard to put this into words, but I saw the vision through feeling it, and the feeling was very warm and good. That international chorus welled up again, praying for my safe return. I can't tell you how important that vision was to me. It gave me the courage to go on.[4]

After completing his own mission, Captain Thomas Hanford, a veteran fighter pilot from the 510th Fighter Squadron, remained in

151

Bosnian airspace to the very limits of his fuel reserves, continuing to search for O'Grady's radio beacon. On June 8 he picked up O'Grady's faint signal. Within hours, a rescue force made up of more than forty aircraft and scores of Marines was on its way to extract O'Grady.

Several days later Captain O'Grady arrived at Andrews Air Force Base aboard an Air Force C-20. Getting off the plane, he particularly noticed the big banner:

BASHER 52
America's Been Praying
Welcome Home,
Scott O'Grady

N O T E S

CHAPTER 1: EPIMENIDES OF CRETE

1. Diogenes Laertius, *The Lives of Eminent Philosophers*, Loeb Classical Library, trans. R.D. Hicks (London: Harvard University Press, 1925), vol. 1, 110.
2. Don Richardson, *Eternity in Their Hearts* (Ventura, Calif.: Regal, 1981), 9-25.
3. Merrill C. Tenney, ed. *The New Pictorial Encyclopedia of the Bible*, (Grand Rapids, Mich.: Zondervan, 1974), vol. 4, 177-78.
4. F.F. Bruce, *Commentary on the Book of the Acts, New International Commentary on the New Testament* (Grand Rapids, Mich.: Eerdmans, 1986), 359-60.

OTHER SOURCES:
J.H. Freese, trans., *The Art of Rhetoric*, Book 3, 17:10. Loeb Classical Library (Cambridge, Mass.: Harvard University Press).

CHAPTER 2: ALEXANDER THE GREAT

1. Merrill C. Tenney, *New Testament Survey* (Grand Rapids, Mich.: Eerdmans, 1953), 16.
2. *The World Book Encyclopedia*, vol. 1 (Chicago: Field Enterprises, 1967), 324.
3. *Nelson's Illustrated Bible Dictionary* (Nashville: Nelson, 1986), 34.
4. *World Book*, vol. 1, 324.
5. *World Book*, vol. 1, 324.
6. Flavius Josephus, *Antiquities of the Jews*, XI, vii, 5.
7. Josephus, XI, vii, 3.
8. Josephus, XI, vii, 3.
9. Josephus, XI, vii, 4-5.
10. *World Book*, vol. 1, 325.
11. Tenney, 15.

CHAPTER 3: ABGARUS

1. Eusebius Pamphilius, *Ecclesiastical History* (Grand Rapids, Mich.: Baker, 1981), 44-45.
2. Eusebius, 45.
3. Eusebius, 45-46.
4. William Cureton, *Ancient Syriac Documents Relative to the Earliest Establishment of Christianity in Edessa* (London: Williams and Norgate, 1864), 6.

CHAPTER 5: FLAVIUS VALERIUS CONSTANTINUS

1. Eusebius Pamphilius, *The Life of Constantine the Great*, as quoted in *Nicene and Post-Nicene Fathers of the Christian Church*, 2nd series, ed. Philip Schaff and Henry Wace (New York: 1890; Grand Rapids, Mich.: Eerdmans, 1952), vol. 1:363-64, 489-93.

OTHER SOURCES:

Henry H. Halley, *Halley's Bible Handbook* (Grand Rapids, Mich.: Zondervan, 1978), 759.

Kenneth Scott Latourette, *A History of the Expansion of Christianity* (New York: Harper & Bros., 1937), vol. 1, 158.

Nancy Zinsser Walworth, *Constantine* (New York: Chelsea House, 1989), 13-17, 40-47.

CHAPTER 6: AUGUSTINE OF HIPPO

1. Augustine, *Confessions*, trans. R.S. Pine-Coffin (Harmondsworth: Penguin, 1966), VI, 6.
2. Augustine, VIII, 8.
3. Augustine, VIII, 12.
4. Augustine, IX, 10.

5. Augustine, IX, 1.
6. Michael Marshall, *The Restless Heart* (Grand Rapids, Mich.: Eerdmans, 1987), 86.

CHAPTER 7: PATRICK

1. Charles H.H. Wright, trans., *The Writings of Patrick*, (London: Religious Tract Society), 42.
2. Wright, 42.
3. Wright, 46-47.
4. *The World Book Encyclopedia* (Chicago: Field Enterprises, 1967), vol. 15, 174.

CHAPTER 8: GIOVANNI FRANCESCO BERNARDONE

1. Leonard von Matt and Walter Hauser, *St. Francis of Assisi* (Chicago: Henry Regnery, 1956), 9.
2. T.S.R. Boase, *St. Francis of Assisi* (Bloomington, Ind.: Indiana University Press, 1968), 28.
3. Boase, 28.
4. von Matt, 13.
5. von Matt, 13.

CHAPTER 9: THOMAS AQUINAS

1. Tim Dowley, ed., *Eerdman's Handbook to the History of Christianity* (Grand Rapids, Mich.: Eerdmans, 1977), 288.
2. DeArteaga, William, *Quenching the Spirit* (Lake Mary, Fla.: Creation House, 1992), 75-76.
3. G.K. Chesterton, *St. Thomas Aquinas* (New York: Sheed & Ward, 1933), 172.

CHAPTER 10: JEANNE LA PUCELLE

1. William Shakespeare, *Henry V*, act 4, scene 3.
2. Susan Banfield, *Joan of Arc* (New York: Chelsea House, 1988), 23.
3. Banfield, 25.
4. Banfield, 32.
5. Lucien Fabre, *Joan of Arc*, trans. Gerard Hopkins (New York: McGraw-Hill, 1954), 277-78.
6. Fabre, 279.
7. Fabre, 279.
8. Herbert Thurston, S.J., and Donald Attwater, eds., *Butler's Lives of the Saints* (New York: P.J. Kenedy & Sons, 1956), 427-30.

OTHER SOURCES:

Polly Schoyer Brooks, *Beyond the Myth, the Story of Joan of Arc* (New York: J.B. Lippincott, 1990).

CHAPTER 11: CHRISTOPHER COLUMBUS

1. Christopher Columbus, *Book of Prophecies.* Much of this work has been translated by August J. Kling, who quoted these excerpts in an article in *The Presbyterian Layman*, October 1971.
2. Peter Marshall and David Manuel, *The Light and the Glory* (Old Tappan, N.J.: Revell, 1977), 62-63.
3. Bjorn Landstrom, *Columbus* (New York: Macmillan, 1966), 37-38.
4. Marshall and Manuel, 64-66.

CHAPTER 12: BLAISE PASCAL

1. Robert Maynard Hutchins, ed., Pascal (Encyclopedia Britannica, Inc., 1952), v-vi.

2. Morris Bishop, *Pascal, the Life of Genius* (Westport, Conn.: Greenwood, 1964), 168.
3. Bishop, 171.
4. Bishop, 171.
5. Bishop, 173.
6. Bishop, 173-74.

CHAPTER 13: JOHN WESLEY

1. Dowley, 447-48.
2. Dowley, 448.
3. William J. Petersen and Warner A. Hutchinson, eds., *The Heart of Wesley's Journal* (New Canaan, Conn.: Keats, 1979), 146.

CHAPTER 14: GEORGE FRIDERIC HANDEL

SOURCES:

Charles Ludwig, *George Frideric Handel* (Milford, Mich.: Mott Media, 1987), 157-58.

Patrick Kavanaugh, *The Spiritual Lives of Great Composers* (Nashville: Sparrow, 1992), 3.

CHAPTER 15: CAPTAIN GEORGE WASHINGTON

1. Norma Cournow Camp, *George Washington* (Milford, Mich.: Mott Media, 1977), 58.
2. Camp, 59.
3. George Bancroft, *History of the United States of America*, vol. 3 (Boston: Little, Brown, 1879), 124.
4. Bancroft, 120-125.
5. Camp, 58-65.

6. William J. Johnson, *George Washington, the Christian* (Nashville: Abingdon, 1919), 23-28.

CHAPTER 16: GENERAL GEORGE WASHINGTON

1. Richard Wheeler, *Voices of 1776* (Greenwich: Fawcett Premier, 1972), 288.
2. George Washington, "The Valley Forge Oration," as quoted in Verna M. Hall, *The Christian History of the American Revolution* (San Francisco: Foundation for American Christian Education, 1975), 61.
3. Wesley Braushaw, *The National Tribune*, December 1880 (Washington, D.C.: The National Tribune Company).

CHAPTER 17: CHARLES GRANDISON FINNEY

1. Ken Curtis, ed., "Maker of Modern Revivalism," *Christian History*, November 1988, 2-3
2. Charles G. Finney, *Charles G. Finney* (Old Tappan, N.J.: Revell, 1908), 4-5.
3. Finney, 7.
4. Finney, 14.
5. Finney, 15.
6. Finney, 17.
7. Finney, 17.
8. Finney, 19.
9. Finney, 19-21.
10. Finney, 22-23.
11. Finney, 24-25.

CHAPTER 18: HARRIET TUBMAN

1. Sarah Bradford, *Harriet, the Moses of Her People* (Gloucester, Mass.: Corinth, 1961), 32-33.
2. Thomas Garrett, as quoted in Bradford, 76.
3. Bradford, 79.
4. Bradford, 23-24.
5. Bradford, 24-25.
6. Quoted in Bradford, 114-15.
7. Bradford, 74.
8. Bradford, 93.
9. Bradford, 128-29.

CHAPTER 19: HARRIET BEECHER STOWE

1. Norma Johnson, *Harriet* (New York: Four Winds, 1994), 55.
2. Johnson, 56.
3. Johnson, 63-64.
4. Johnson, 134.
5. Johnson, 136.
6. Johnson, 137.
7. Charles Edward Stowe, *Life of Harriet Beecher Stowe* (New York: Houghton, Mifflin, 1889), 149.
8. Bradford, 42-43.

CHAPTER 20: ABRAHAM LINCOLN

1. William J. Johnson, *Abraham Lincoln the Christian* (Milford, Mich.: Mott Media, 1976), 37.
2. Carl Sandburg, *Abraham Lincoln* (New York: Charles Scribner's Sons, 1950), vol. 5, 378.

3. Lincoln's Second Inaugural Address, 1864.
4. Charles Chiniquy, as quoted in Johnson, 136-43.
5. Ward Hill Lamon, *Recollection of Abraham Lincoln* (Chicago: A.C. McClurg & Co., 1911).
6. Johnson, 182.

CHAPTER 21: GEORGE WASHINGTON CARVER

1. David Collins, *George Washington Carver* (Milford, Mich.: Mott Media, 1981), 105-106.
2. *The New Encyclopedia Britannica* (Encyclopedia Britannica, Inc., 1992), vol.2, 913.

CHAPTER 22: NORMAN VINCENT PEALE

1. Norman Vincent Peale, *The Positive Power of Jesus Christ* (Wheaton, Ill.: Tyndale House, 1980), 48.
2. Peale, 49.
3. Peale, 50.
4. Peale, 51.
5. Peale, 51.
6. Peale, 51-52.
7. Peale, 53.

CHAPTER 23: CATHERINE MARSHALL

1. Catherine Marshall, *Meeting God at Every Turn* (Carmel, N.Y.: Guideposts, 1980), 13.
2. Marshall, 98.

3. Marshall, 100.
4. Marshall, 98-99.
5. Marshall, 100.
6. Marshall, 100-101.

CHAPTER 24: ELIZABETH TEN BOOM

1. Carole C. Carlson, *Corrie ten Boom: Her Life, Her Faith* (Old Tappan, N.J.: Revell, 1984), 109.
2. Corrie ten Boom, *The Hiding Place* (Washington Depot, Conn.: Chosen, 1971), 176.

CHAPTER 25: MARTIN LUTHER KING, JR.

1. Allen Johnson, et al., eds., *Dictionary of American Biography* (New York: Charles Scribner's Sons, 1988), 232-33.
2. Martin Luther King, Jr., *Stride Toward Freedom* (San Francisco: Harper & Row, 1958), 41-43.
3. King, 134-35.

CHAPTER 26: NORMAN WILLIAMS

1. Norman Williams with George Otis, *Terror at Tenerife* (Medford, Ore.: Omega, 1977), 43.
2. Williams, 59.
3. Williams, 20.
4. Williams, 60-63.
5. Williams, 20, 64-65.

Chapter 27: "Pistol" Pete Maravich

1. Curry Kirkpatrick, "A Singular Showman," *Sports Illustrated*, January 18, 1988, 9.
2. Pete Maravich and Darrel Campbell, *Heir to a Dream* (Nashville: Nelson, 1987), 191-93.

Chapter 28: Vladimir Slolvev, Oleg Atkov, and Leonod Kiaim

1. *Miracles Are Heaven Sent* (Tulsa, Okla.: Honor Books, 1995), 150.

Chapter 29: Dennis Byrd

1. Dennis Byrd with Michael D'Orso, *Rise and Walk* (New York: Harper Collins, 1993), 130-31.
2. Byrd, 211.

OTHER SOURCES:
Dennis Byrd and Susan Reed, "Walking on Air," *People Weekly*, September 13, 1993, 98-108.
David Gelman, "The Most Dangerous Game," *Newsweek*, December 14, 1992, 66.
Peter King, "He Has the Strength," *Sports Illustrated*, December 14, 1992, 22-27.

Chapter 30: Captain Scott O'Grady

1. Scott O'Grady with Jeff Coplon, *Return with Honor* (New York: Doubleday, 1995), 89.
2. O'Grady, 141-42.
3. O'Grady, 110.
4. O'Grady, 116.

OTHER SOURCES:

Bruce Auster and Samantha Power, "One Amazing Kid," *U.S. News & World Report*, June 19, 1995, 40-44.

Kevin Fedarko, "Glomming on to a Hero," *Time*, June 26, 1995, 30-32.

Cathy Free, "On Tour with Scott O'Grady," *People Weekly*, January 15, 1996, 37.

Richard Jerome, Andrew Marton, and Mary Esselman, "Hero's Welcome," *People Weekly*, June 26, 1995, 50-52.